DIARY IN BLUE.

By Steve Cartwright.

Caution: Some realistic, rough "street" language.

CONTENTS..

DARK.

THE WRONG PLACE TO ROB.

BARRICADED GUNMAN.

JUST AN OLD MAN ON HIS PORCH.

JUST ONE MORE STEP.

LAST THOUGHT.

HERE'S LOOKING AT YOU.

DETECTIVE DAYS:

LABOR DISPUTE.

VALLEY OF TINY LIGHTS.

UNCLE CHARLIE.

SHOTS FIRED.

DESCENT INTO THE UNDERWORLD.

"YOU MAY THINK I'M SOME KINDA NUT."

ROBBERY STAKEOUT.

YOU DON'T PAY HER.

A SLIME OF PASSION.

LISTENER SANDWICH.

MUDDY THE WATERS.

TALE FROM THE CRYPT.

ANTICIPATION IS THE HARDEST THING.

VISITOR.

NEWS DAYS.

When I was a newspaper reporter, I looked like Rasputin. It was 1974 and I was eighteen with long black hair parted in the middle.

I supplemented my income writing the news by delivering the *South Fulton News-Daily*. The pay was deplorable but I was in love with writing. The big Atlanta daily, the *Constitution*, paid a monthly stipend for what journalists call a stringer, a non-staff writer who contributes crime stories. And I sold to other Atlanta publications, such as *Creative Loafing.*

Seeing my words in print thrilled me, and still does. My editor was Ken, a skirt-chasing man of forty whose mustache had grown in red on one side and brown on the other. He must have been kidding when he called me to his desk in our little storefront office. "I want you to cover cops," he said.

"I don't even like cops," I mumbled.

"You see the word `News' in our rag's title? Crime is news. You're our new cop shop reporter."

Ken's eyes followed me as I loped back to my littered desk. Taking the phone, I called the local police departments. "I'm Steve Cartwright with the *News-Daily*. Anything going on?"

"Not that I know of," whoever answered the phone said.

When the competing paper covered a bank robbery and I didn't, Ken raised hell. "Goddamn it, Cartwright! I told you to cover the cops! You can't do it from a desk! Get your ass to the cop shops and make some contacts!"

East Point, the town of my birth, was a community nestled next to Atlanta on the southside. Atlanta was a city cut out of the forest. Skyscrapers and city lights pierced its sky. It boasted of a population of 393,929, its international airport, 55 hospitals and 37 schools of higher learning. The male tourists, however, came here for all the classy, totally-nude bars. Nothing else in Georgia came close to its cosmopolitan veneer, and a visit to Hot-lanta,□ with its bars and nightlife, was a big deal to our country cousins. East Point was (and still is) a suburban city. We were proud of our big sister, yet glad not to have her crime problems. As a first grader in the early '60ies I had toured the East Point police station. It's now vague memories of a motorcycle cop showing us kids his bike; it captivated us when he flicked a button and his siren yelped, his blue lights flashed.

He showed us a black-and-white photo of a man looking into the camera with half-lidded eyes, a big round hole in his chest.

"What's this?" I asked.

"A bullet wound. The man's common-law wife shot him."

We all looked closer, not understanding that the man was a corpse.

In the jail cells upstairs, the cop quickly ushered us past a prisoner who was taking a dump on the commode in his cell.

The tour almost over, my teacher stopped me from going to the white porcelain drinking fountain. "You use that one," she said, pointing to a new metal one.

"Why can't I use this one?" I asked.

"Can't you read? The sign there says this is the colored drinking fountain."

When I entered the building as a reporter a decade-and-a-half later, I looked for the Colored☐ drinking fountain, but it was gone.

Conscious that I must look like a hippie to all the crew-cut cops passing in the hall, I was relieved to see a short, big-bellied cop, a soggy cigar jutting from his mouth. He was Pete Miller. His dad, Bing, had been my little league football coach. When I told him that, he snatched the cigar from his mouth and vigorously shook my hand. "Did you know my dad had a leg amputated?" he asked.

"No. Is he all right?"

"You know Bing, hoss. Nothing slows the old geezer down. He's got a wooden leg."

Pete became my friend. Within a month my hair was as short as his. Every day I haunted the police station. Chatting in the desk sergeant's office, I saw cops hauling in a parade of drunks, some not too gently.

A preacher from a halfway house breezed in one afternoon. "Boys," he declared in a deep basso voice, addressing the miserable souls in the drunk tank. "You know that an alcoholic loses five-thousand brain cells a day?"

Being an avid reader, I couldn't resist blurting: "*Everyone* loses five-thousand brain cells a day. It's a natural process."

Looking askance at me, the preacher hissed: "I'm trying to save souls here, son!"

"Steve," Pete called from the desk in the middle of the book-in room. "Our Auto Theft detective's doin' a search warrant at a used car lot." Nodding toward his police walkie-talkie, he continued: "Sounds like he's got summin big. Buncha cars comin' back signal forty-fives." The cops were already talking coptalk to me, just like I was one of them. "You wanna go?"

"Sounds like a story to me."

"Let's go." Thinking I would drive over in my unreliable clunker, I headed for the front door. "This way, hoss," Pete said and I followed him to his patrol car.

That metallic beast sat in the summer sun, all mystery and foreboding. "Get in, hoss," Pete said. "We gotta get there quick."

Settling uneasily in on the passenger side, I was all too conscious of the metal screen behind me. Pete flipped on his blue lights and siren and we went flying out of the driveway. Traffic was pulling over as Pete flew down the streets that suddenly seemed unfamiliar to me. It was as though I were entering another world.

Pete pulled onto the sidewalk in front of a small used VW lot. I saw five marked units, blue lights throbbing, and three black detective cars, all parked haphazardly as if they hit the place fast.

Following Pete like a puppy, we went to

where Gerald Jackson was checking a VIN on a Beatle. "You need me to help, hoss?" Pete asked the Auto Theft detective.

"Yeah, Pete. I've got hits on about four cars so far. What this guy's been doing is putting stolen parts on his cars -- so I've gotta check a lot of parts."

Pete had me call parts numbers off to him while he, after snapping his soggy cigar into his mouth, jotted a list into his notepad.

The lot owner, a fortyish man with a black pompadour, suddenly went into a rant. Pointing at me, he exclaimed: "Are you a cop?"

"No," I stammered, feeling like an imposter. "I'm a reporter." It was like I didn't want to say the word.

"Then *you* get off my propitty 'fore I take a crowbar to your head!"

"You want to prosecute him for threatening you?" asked Officer Bob Matthews.

This was bad – a reporter should not

become part of the story he's covering.

****

By that time I was going to crime scenes everyday.

A College Park cop phoned me at the newspaper office with a tip: "A nasty 44 / 48 at a jewelry store."

I zoomed out the door, heading for my dark-blue Belaire.

A crowd stood outside the little store on Main Street. Two cops were already there, pushing everybody back. The adrenaline rush churned my blood.

Feeling uncomfortable, I stayed close to a cop I knew as he entered the front door. A detective was in the back room, visible through a door as he examined something on the floor.

An ID tech came in to take photos. None of the cops objected to my presence there as I pulled my steno pad from my back blue jeans pocket and began note-taking.

A middle-aged woman, weeping, face flushed, told a detective: "These two black boys came in and one pulled a knife and demanded the money. We gave 'em everything we had in the cash register, then they told us to go in the back and lay down on the floor. We did just what they told us to do, then, for no reason, one of 'em stabbed Celeste. Just kept stabbing her in the back. Is she going to be all right?" No one answered her and she looked toward the door where we could still see the other detective.

In a few minutes, an ambulance arrived and the two EMTs went to the back room. Celeste was dead. They carried her body out on a gurney, completely covered by a white sheet.

Feeling awkward, I went outside where the air seemed fresher.

A boy, maybe eleven, was speaking

loudly, "I heard the place got robbed. Heard they killed one of the clerks." He was talking very confidently, but when the EMTs came out with the gurney, and a foot with a green shoe slipped from beneath the sheet, the kid suddenly went hysterical, screaming, crying, and ran away.

****

There would be more murders. By the time I covered the bludgeoning of an old woman, I was dressing, talking, and acting like a cop. It was a bug I would later see other reporters succumb to.

When the East Point detectives hauled in their suspect, the old lady's tall, thin maid, none of them told me to leave. I was one of the guys. The maid, who the old lady's family hired from a halfway house, denied killing her boss.

"Then why are your bloody footprints on the kitchen floor?" Detective Sonny Lowery exclaimed, his face right up against the fiftyish woman's pale cheeks. "The old lady's body was at her kitchen table. She was reading her Bible when you came up behind her and started beating her in the head with a hammer."

Her eyes avoiding his, she shook her head.

"You beat her so long and so hard her blood ran down your legs and into your shoes," the detective shouted, getting in even closer, making the woman squirm. "We got your shoes. They're full of blood!"

"I'm on my period," she blurted.

"The blood in your shoes is from the old woman!"

"Alfred Hitchcock is a friend of mine and he wouldn't let me pull off such a botched murder." She was a twenty-four, I realized.

****

A signal twenty-four. I talked like a cop. I looked like a cop. But I was supposed to be a newspaper reporter.

Soon I was attending choir practice. That's what cops called drinking sessions done after they got off-duty. No other civilian, except sometimes females, police groupies, were invited.

Choir practice was used to let off steam. They passed war stories around like a whiskey bottle. It was a group of mostly young cops with testosterone popping like six-shooters.

"I got a twenty-four call tonight," a patrolman said, sipping a bottle of Bud. It was midnight and about six of us had gathered in the lower police parking lot, standing under the moon. "It was at the Holiday Inn. The twenty-four was this man. He was running up and down the hall naked. I get there and he runs as

soon as he sees me. Runs back to his room.
Inside his room he's pulled the shades off of all
the lamps and he's spread hamburger meat on
them. He's yelling that he has to do that to
neutralize the sparrow-keets."

"What's a sparrow-keet?" his sergeant
asked, mixing bourbon and Coca-Cola in a
plastic cup.

"Dunno, Sarge. Maybe part-sparrow and
part-parakeet. Maybe he saw them flying
around him or something."

We all laughed. Sometime later I would
read about spirochete, a bacteria that causes
syphilis.

"Sonny," I asked the detective with the
Dirty Harry coif. "How'd you figure out the maid
killed that old lady?"

Smirking, cigarette smoke wafting from
his nostrils, he boasted: "Good detective work,
hoss. Good detective work."

It was then I decided I wanted to do

good detective work, to become a cop. A big-city, Atlanta cop. Something similar to a spirochete had entered my blood. Something strong enough to make me abandon -- temporarily -- my love of writing.

I wanted to go straight to being a Homicide detective. But things don't work that way on APD.

PATROL DAYS.

CONTEMPLATING YELLOW CRIME SCENE TAPE.

A street person had been killed in a knife fight. The zone sergeant rolled up in the twilight and ordered my training officer to secure the area with yellow crime scene tape, which we quickly did.

I was a rookie cop, riding with a training officer in 1978, after six months in the Atlanta Police Department's recruit school. They made us jog and exercise until I was trim, fit, and clean cut.

A crowd of gawkers and reporters assembled at the scene of the murder. I recognized some of the members of the fourth estate. Only a year ago I had been where they were now. It was like I'd come from an alien world.

As my training officer tied off the last bit of tape, I suddenly found myself saying to the crowd: "Everybody back away from the crime scene."

Something stirred within me as I passed under the tape. As a reporter I could never breech the tape. Now I could!

Passing under the barrier again, I was feeling the power of my new position.

My ex-colleagues stood outside. I stood inside.

I passed under the yellow crime scene tape again. And again.

A LESSON IN LOVE.

While still a rookie in field training, I learned an ugly truth about domestic violence.

My Field Training Officer's beat was in a squalid locale in southeast Atlanta. As I followed him from the patrol car that night to the porch of the dilapidated house, he cautioned: "Be careful, rook. Domestic fight calls are when cops get whacked most often. I've been attacked before trying to arrest a boyfriend who battered his old lady. It was his old lady who attacked me."

I found that hard to believe. Why would the very woman we're trying to help attack us? But, as we stepped onto the wooden porch, I didn't voice my doubt. Could be this old vet was just jaded.

"I know you may find that hard to believe," he said, as if reading my mind, "but you have to understand the woman usually loves the guy. He's usually the one who brings in money for her and the kids. It's hard to comprehend sometimes."

Above the rotting front door, a single yellow

bulb glowed in the winter gloom.

"Don't step in the blood."

"What blood?" I exclaimed, stopping.

"There," he replied, pointing his flashlight to the floor where a puddle of bright blood was freezing in the cold December air.

Without knocking or calling out, the old vet opened the front door and walked in. How arrogant, I thought, how intrusive. I wondered if I should refuse to follow. But I tagged along, wondering if this was an unlawful entry.

"Don't step on the bloody scissors. They might be evidence."

"What bloody scissors?!"

Sighing as though he were saddled with the stupidest rook in the world, he pointed to the hallway floor. There I spotted a pair of open scissors dripping with red liquid. Next to it was a piece of wall molding freshly torn from the wall, its nails projecting upward.

"What the hell you doin' in my mutherfuckin' house?" a black male, about twenty-five, wearing a soiled tee-shirt and green pants, exclaimed angrily, rushing toward us down the hall. He stopped five feet from us, but I could smell the booze.

"We got a call here you're beatin' your old lady," the old vet said as if it were no big deal. Wondering if this guy was going to attack us, I debated pulling my nightstick, or my gun. My FTO stood his ground, not menacing, but holding his metal flashlight as if its only function was to illuminate the darkness. I, of course, knew better.

"Get out my mutherfuckin' house!"

"After we see your old lady's all right, we'll go. So where is she?"

"She ain't here. Went to the sto'."

"On a cold night like this? Say, what store's open around here this time uh night? Come on, man, let us see she's all right and we can go. She *is* all right, ain't she?"

Peeking into the next room, I saw two older black males watching *the Tonight Show With Johnny Carson.* They were taking great pains to ignore us.

"You ain't got nar'n mutherfuckin' wer'nt!"

"I don't need a warrant to insure your old lady's safe. Now, where is she?" He stepped toward the irate man, and I knew all hell was gonna break loose, but the man stepped aside. I cautiously followed, while the drunk's tirade continued, almost unintelligible.

"Where's your mamma?" the vet asked, looking into a room where four small, scared kids stood huddled.

Looking around my FTO, I saw the youngest innocently say: "She in they bedroom. My daddy whooped up on her."

"Shut yore mutherfuckin' mouth, boy!"

Quickly laying his hand against the man's chest, the vet warned: "I won't tolerate you talking to a child like that."

"You cain't bust me in my own mutherfuckin' house!"

"Don't try me, man. Just step back and chill out."

I followed him into a bedroom illuminated only by a naked bulb hanging on a cord from the ceiling. The place was the messiest room I'd ever seen. It reeked of cigarette smoke, booze, dirt, and rotted food. In the dim light, I could see roaches scurrying over the naked floor.

"I just heard a moan," I exclaimed. "Sounded like it was far away. There! I heard it again." The bed was covered with several pounds of dirty clothes, but this was where I heard the moaning. Quickly tossing clothes from the bed, I unearthed a black woman lying on her belly and moaning in pain. Lifting her by her shoulder, I saw the pillow she lay on was saturated with blood. A strand of silver saliva stretched from her mouth to the pillow like a string. The wound to her left cheek was deep and dripping blood. It was among old scars already healed.

"Call an ambulance, rook, and you, man, are under arrest."

As I called an ambulance over my handie-talkie, my FTO quickly cuffed the husband and was leading him out the door.

The woman sat up in bed and screamed: "Where he takin' my husband?"

"Don't worry, ma'am," I assured her. "He won't be able to hurt you anymore. We're taking him to jail."

"No! You cain't lock up my husband! I love my husband!"

I was dumbfounded. "Isn't he the one who stabbed you in your face?"

She nodded rapidly, tears flowing and mingling with her oozing blood.

"And you don't want to prosecute him for it?"

"No! Bring him back!"

My FTO heard her and silently began unlocking the cuffs. To her, he said: "An ambulance'll be here in a few minutes. They'll take you to Grady. We'll make a report about the call. Let's go, rook."

"Go?" I asked, confused.

"She doesn't want to prosecute," he said with a shrug. "There's nothing more we can do."

That was in 1978. Since then domestic violence laws have changed in Georgia, and we could now have arrested the batterer whether the victim wanted us to or not.

As we exited, the old vet said: "It don't matter now if you step on those scissors or not. We won't be using them as evidence."

MORNING WATCH UNIFORM PATROL.

After six weeks of riding with Field Training Officers in three different precincts, I got my permanent assignment: Zone 2 morning watch.

Morning watch is the graveyard shift. The Zone

2 precinct covered the northeast quadrant of this city of 131 square miles. Its southern sector was in the hellhole of the inner city. Northside was the prestigious Buckhead community where mansions and trendy bars lit the night.

Coming on an hour before midnight, we working southside caught barroom brawls, prowlers, pimps and their hookers. APD made most DUI cases on this watch.

Alone in a patrol car on a slow night, I was bored. Too new to the zone to have a regular beat, I was a roustabout, ☐ filling in for vets when they were off. It was after 2:00 A.M. when I spotted the mud-splattered pickup truck stopped alone at a green traffic light on Ponce de Leon Ave.

Curious, I watched as the light turned red, then green again. The truck never moved.

Driving next to the pickup, I saw the driver, a lone white male wearing a cowboy hat, passed out against the steering wheel. Willie Nelson boomed from the radio speakers.

Pulling forward, then turning around, I stopped behind the obviously drunk driver, and turned on my flashing blue ights.

Walking forward, I opened the door of the truck and nudged the redneck. He didn't stir. Nudging him again, he snapped away from the wheel.

"Step out of the truck, please," I ordered, and he jerked his face my way. He looked disoriented, then eyed my uniform with dread.

Suddenly he reached under his seat with his right hand. I reacted immediately, snatching him out and throwing him to the pavement. His Stetson shot from his long red hair as he struggled. Pinning his beefy arms behind his back, I quickly cuffed him and pulled him to his feet.

"You motherfuckin' cop!" he spat in a cloud of Jack Daniels as I locked him into the back of my patrol car. "I hate fuckin' cops!"

Returning to the idling pickup truck, I shined my flashlight to see what he had been reaching for beneath his seat.

It was a Smith & Wesson .44 Magnum, fully loaded.

This was one of the many pecks on the cheek I got in my career, but not the full Kiss of Death.

TROUBLED SON, TROUBLED MOTHER.

APD had been in a lawsuit over hiring and my recruit class was the first hiring the federal court allowed in five years. The manpower was dangerously low. Our dispatcher would routinely call and advise: "Pull over and write down these eight calls I'm sending you on."

So when I heard this call for me around 1 AM, I knew I'd probably be on my own: "Unit 208, see the woman about a 24-violent." But, when I arrived at the tiny bugalow, Officer Larry Gilbert was already there, although he was still technically on another call. Larry was there to assist the new rookie. Just the night before, we'd responded to a broken door at a mom-n-pop store; we searched inside and found the perps gone; while awaiting the owner, Larry took a Milky Way bar from the shelf and ate it, after leaving coins for it next to the cash register.

Knocking at the bungalow, I saw a woman in a house coat open the door and beckon us in. "My son Sean's a damn dope fiend and I want you to take him to Juvvie! Sean! Sean, come in here right now!"

Within seconds, a boy of sixteen walked in and halted when he saw two cops.

"Go on, officers! I'm a single mother and I can't control him! He's probably high right now! Take him to Juvvie!"

He was a little guy and when I saw him ball his fists, I gripped my metal flashlight in my left hand; I had learned in the academy to always leave my gunhand empty.

Larry spoke up as I stood there speechless: "Sean. Come outside."

"You gonna arrest me? What for?"

"We're just gonna talk."

Walking outside, closing the door, Larry directed us into a pool of yellow light cast by a gas lamp. "Sean," he said in a suddenly kind voice. "I had a stepmother who abused me, physically and mentally."

Both Sean and I looked like we'd been slapped. I don't know if Larry was telling the truth or he was being a veteran cop telling Sean what he needed to hear, but Sean's glower turned into a look of wide-eyed amazement.

"Sean, I can tell your mother's . . . a little crazy."

Sean spoke with a trembling voice, no longer trying to portray a tough guy. "My dad abandoned us when I was a baby. Mom had to raise me alone. I *know* it's been tough on her, but what she says -- I don't do drugs."

"I believe you," Larry said, looking directly at him and I could hear the gas hissing from the black lamp. "I didn't get along with my stepmom, either. I'd get so mad at her I just wanted, sometimes, to punch her in the face. She made my life miserable, Sean, but I didn't do anything stupid that would get me in trouble with the law, because once you've been arrested, Sean, even as a juvenile, it starts you on a bad path you might never get off of."

I was as speechless as Sean because I, too, had a stepmother as a kid who abused me physically and mentally.

"Sean," Larry said, laying his hand on the troubled kid's shoulder. "I tolerated my stepmother until I was legally of age to join the military, then I got out of that house and *never* went back. Will you make me a promise, Sean? No matter *what* your crazy mother does or says, you'll be cool, and when you're of age to leave home, you will, and you'll live your own life?"

Sean was crying. Larry was crying. I was crying.

REACTION.

By the end of our tour of duty we still had not heard about the cop-killer in Zone 1 being snatched up. We hadn't taken care of business and we felt restless.

As we gathered at the top of the hill where the precinct stood, the dawning sun was trapped behind thick, gray clouds. The world looked especially frigid because of the snow on the ground.

"I heard he came into a convenience store and a thirty-six was going down," said Larry Gilbert. "The perp turned, saw the uniform, and shot him in the gut with his shotgun. Then the perp ran out, didn't even get the money, left Johnson bleeding out on the floor."

There were a dozen of us patrolmen standing in the snow at the top of the hill. Our shift was over, but no one felt like leaving. No one felt like talking.

What words could we say? We had patrolled all night, anxiously awaiting word that Homicide had snatched the cop-killer. We each hoped that we could be the one to bust him. If he resisted, we would gladly kill him, for he had needlessly taken one of our own.

Lighting a cigarette, blowing smoke into the bleak air, I looked at my buddies in their blue uniforms. Silence.

Then a snowball hit me in the head, saturating my black hair.

Stunned, I and my buddies looked for the assailant.

"There he is! Jones!" In the lower part of the precinct parking lot, an officer was quickly scooping another snowball from a parked car. He lobbed it at us, missing, but suddenly we were boys again playing in the snow.

Cops were scooping up snowballs and throwing them at each other, whooping, yelling, laughing. Action, at last.

Reaction to stress and grief is often a strange thing, but when I drove home that morning I felt better.

HAUNTED PRECINCT.

"I was working in the old Zone 2 precinct alone one Saturday afternoon," recalled Officer Kit Carson, fumbling with his thick, black mustache. "My head was lowered while I read something on my desk, and out of my peripheral vision I saw a big cop in a light-blue summer uniform shirt walk up the hall and turn left toward the rollcall room.

"Then it hit me -- we had switched to the dark blue summer uniform shirts, so who could that officer have been? I got up and walked into the rollcall room and there was no one there. Now, I'm not necessarily saying it was Sam Guy's ghost, but whoever I saw was built like him and no one was in the precinct but me."

Sam Guy was a muscle-builder. He had been killed in a shootout while working an extra job at a hotel. His murder was solved many years later.

TIME SLOWS.

It was around 2:00 A.M.

Billy Carter, unit 207, had gotten a fight call at a bar as I was pulling into the city shop to gas up my patrol car. Before I could insert the gas nozzle, Carter's excited voice came over the radio: "Start me another car, Radio!"

I froze, listening, as the dispatcher responded: "Be advised, two-oh-seven, every unit is out of service." Squeezing the nozzle as if it were my .38, gas spurted onto my pants leg.

"They're surrounding me like Indians, Radio! I need some more units!"

He was on the other side of town, but I threw the gas nozzle to the pavement and jumped into my patrol car. With blue lights flashing and siren wailing, I went screeching out of the shop. The smell of gas from my leg was thick in the small space.

"Fifty-nine right away, Radio!" Carter radioed, the signal for an officer-needs-help.

"Two-ten to Radio, I'm responding!" I radioed. "Coming from the shop!"

No one else was responding, as all the cops in the zone were tied up on calls, and I was a long way off.

Carter's exclamation "Fifty-nine RIGHT AWAY!" made me press the petal to the floor. My squad car was flying, but I was still far away.

Popping red lights, screeching around curves, the sweat was dribbling off my forehead.

"Where's my backup, Radio?" Carter gasped over the radio, and I gunned the car even faster. Glancing at the speedometer, I saw I was doing seventy down a residential street. Then I lost it. Going too fast around a curve on North Highland Avenue, my squad car was hurtling almost out of control, over the center line, into the wrong lane.

Thank God there was no opposing traffic, but I hit the brake and everything slowed down. Slowed down miraculously in my mind. My squad car was still hurtling toward the sidewalk out of my control, but everything seemed so slow, like in a dream.

I bounced onto the sidewalk, foot came off the brake a fraction of a second to try and gain control of the wheel, then evening out, barreling down the sidewalk, then pressing the brake almost through the floor.

Time still seemed to be slow, molasses, as my car's heading for the telephone pole, my foot darts from the brake, my hands tug at the wheel, right, right, then foot back on the brake petal, maybe I'm gonna miss that damn telephone pole.

Narrowly avoiding front-ending the pole, I think I've safely skirted the thing, and I seem to be able to see every splinter of the wood, every staple where people have tacked posters for lost dogs and yard sales.

Then I'm jostled as the rear quarter panel kisses the pole, catapulting my squad car back into the street where I finally, after a hundred yards, come to rest.

Time back in. Time returns to normal, and I exhaled, my seat belt clutching me to the seat like a lover.

"Two-ten," I radioed, "I've been involved in an accident."

Jumping from the battered car, adrenaline still rushing, I radioed to Carter: "What's your situation, two-oh-seven?"

"We've got it under control now, thanks."

In a few minutes my sarge arrived, as did Carter, who had two prisoners in the cage of his squad car.

"What happened with your help call?" I asked."When I heard you say you wrecked, I got mad as hell, adrenaline kicked in, and I snatched up these drunk rednecks. Shoved their asses into my car so I could come check on you. You hurt?"

"No. I'm fine." But my hands were still shaking. I couldn't get the episode out of my mind, how time slowed and the calmness that washed over me. I would later experience the same slowness of time in a shootout. Several other cops have told me that they, too, have experienced this phenomenon during a crisis.

PURSUIT?

I drove my squad car very slowly because all of

Atlanta was a sheet of ice.

Even inside the car my breath came out as white clouds. It was only midnight, so I expected the temperature to get even colder before my tour of the morning watch ended.

The heater was already blasting out at me, but I was still miserable. Getting out of this relatively warm car to write a traffic ticket was not what I wanted to do. But when a red compact car in front of me on Cheshire Bridge Rd ran a red light, I knew I had to act.

Getting behind the Toyota, I flipped the toggle for my blue light, but the driver didn't stop.

"Radio," I transmitted to the zone dispatcher, "I've got a Toyota that won't stop. Check the tag." We weren't speeding, probably due to the icy streets, but the driver just wasn't stopping.

"Tag's not stolen," the dispatcher responded in a few seconds, also giving me the registration information.

To myself, I muttered: "Well, there's some

reason they're not pulling over for the blue light." I switched the yelp-siren on and the Toyota's brake lights immediately flared.

Cutting off the siren, throwing the cruiser into PARK, I leaped out and slipped and slid to the stopped vehicle, hand on the butt of my holstered .38.

Instead of desperadoes, it was a solitary woman of about thirty. Maybe she was drunk.

"What's the matter, officer?" she asked in a clear voice.

"Why didn't you stop when I turned the blue light on?" I demanded in my best try-not-to-sound-like-a-rookie voice.

"I haven't seen any blue light," she protested.

"I blue lighted you five blocks back," I said, but my voice trailed off when I gazed back at my squad car. In those days our cars had what was called a bubble gum machine for a blue light. The light was on, but it was not flashing.

Slipping and sliding back to my car, I examined

the bubble gum machine. The cold weather had frozen it.

Boy, did I feel embarrassed.

LEARNED RESPONSE.

"Back when I worked K-9," the veteran cop related to a group over beers at Manuel's Tavern, "my beast and I were working the Peachtree Street Strip.

"There was a parking deck I sometimes used as an observation post. This was on a Saturday afternoon, so the decks were closed. The entrance had a chain drawn across it, and I stepped over the chain and my dog jumped over it.

"We walked up to the next level, and there was a chain drawn across there, too. I stepped over it and my dog jumped over it. The next level was another chain. I stepped over it and he jumped over it.

"On the top level, I walked him to the side where we could look down on Peachtree Street. There was a chain at the edge of the deck, and when he saw that chain he jumped over it like he had the other chains. Luckily I didn't let go of his leash because this chain was to keep cars from driving off the top of the decks. The stupid dog was dangling three stories off the ground! I was finally able to drag him back onto the deck."

JUST AN OLD MAN ON HIS PORCH.

I received a call of someone shooting a gun in a low-rent apartment complex.

Pulling my white cruiser through the witching hour gloom, I saw no people anywhere.

Probably nothing to the call, I decided, cutting the night with my spotlight.

I saw an old man sitting on an apartment porch and figured I'd go ask him if he'd heard any gunshots.

Climbing from my cruiser, I heard a heavy *thunk* from somewhere.

"Excuse me, sir," I said, approaching the elderly black man, my flashlight in my left hand. The raspy lament from a Billie Holliday song played from an A.M. radio hidden in the shadows. "Have you heard anyone shooting a gun?"

He made a stuttering noise.

Routinely illuminating him with my light, I saw a cheap pistol at his feet. I suddenly realized what that thunk sound was I heard as I approached him.

Picking up the gun, I could feel its heat in the

fall cold. "This isn't *your* gun, is it, sir?"

The old guy couldn't get a word out. I abstractly noticed he had no teeth.

"Well, since we don't know who this belongs to, I'll have to turn it in to our Property section. It's probably time for you to go to bed, don't you think?"

"S - Sure is, Officer!" he exclaimed, and was reeling for his open door.

Just a harmless old man, drunk, sitting on his porch, firing a gun into the midnight air.

Luckily for me, death had only brushed me like a feather. He could have shot me as I climbed from my cruiser. In this job you just never know.

BARRICADED GUNMAN.

A fellow patrolman answered a silent alarm call at Capital Cadillac around 4:30 A.M.

"The back door's shattered," he radioed, which caused the troops from Zones 1 and 2 to rush to the downtown dealership. I and four other cops, one armed with a shotgun, entered through the smashed door.

The plan was to go down the corridor and check the offices and showroom for the burglar. While hurrying down the hall, using our flashlights since no lights were on inside, a shot rang out and something pelted my face. It suddenly felt like a sorority of ants were running across my skull. Crouching, I turned to Larry Moore, who was behind me, and I said: "Larry, I think I'm head-shot."

"I think it's just from the plaster board," he said, examining my face with his light. "I don't see any blood." The bullet blasted the wall beside me. Examining the hole, I saw it missed me by inches.

"Shots fired on call," Larry radioed. "We've got a barricaded gunman. Notify SWAT."

"Received," responded the dispatcher. "I'm sending more zone units, also notifying SWAT." This late at night, SWAT officers were off-duty and would have to be called from home.

Wiping wall detritus from my face, I and the others low-walked down the hall to the showroom. Larry Gilbert, toting the only shotgun, found the light switch and flicked it on. Bright lights illuminated the showroom where a dozen Caddies were on display.

"He must be in that office there," Gilbert whispered, pointing to a dark, open door. Gilbert called to the barricaded gunman: "We've got you surrounded! Give yourself up!"

The voice of a young black male responded from the office, some twenty feet from us: "I ain't givin' up! I'm gonna kill myself!"

We fanned out, using the shiny new cars as shields. "Listen," called Gilbert, "you don't need to do anything stupid. How old are you?"

"Seventeen," he called back. "If ya'll rush me I'm gonna kill as many of you pigs as I can." It was

1980 and it was popular to refer to us as pigs.

Radio advised us SWAT's ETA was forty-five minutes.

More cops arrived, several trying to talk the gunman into surrendering, but he always responded by saying we would end up killing him, but he planned to take as many of us with him as he could. After fifteen minutes of this, Gilbert laid his shotgun against a car fender, picked up a tire from a display and, with us looking at him, he exclaimed: "Let's rush him, guys!" He rolled the tire like a bowling ball toward the open door and got behind cover, retrieving his shotgun.

The tire rolled into the door and two shots rang out. We held our positions as the perp evaluated what just happened. "I ain't gonna fall for *that* again," he shouted.

He'd fired three rounds, which meant he probably had three left. Three fewer rounds for him to put into us.

Stretched over the hood of a Caddy, my .38

continually trained at the open door, I realized the gunman could bust through any second, gun blazing.

Time was ticking on and I was wondering when SWAT would arrive and take over from us.

Turning my head for a second, I could see through the storefront window. Across the street, a crowd had gathered.

My gun hand was growing fatigued. I found it interesting that, in this life-or-death situation, it was actually possible for my mind to wander. To think about work I needed to do around the house, about my dogs, about a sexy waitress at a club on my beat --

There was a motion, my senses suddenly heightened, gunfire erupted, more flurries, cops rushing forward, me rushing forward, a figure had dashed from the door, cordite was in the air, the figure was spinning as if gurgling down a drain, and we rushed him, he was writhing on the ground, and someone kicked the revolver from his hand.

It happened that quickly.

One of his hands had been shattered by a shotgun blast, and there wasn't enough left to handcuff. He was alive and none of us were hurt.

Two officers rode in the ambulance with the perp to the Grady ER.

Back in the showroom, detectives from Homicide and Internal Affairs arrived to investigate the shooting. "How many rounds did you fire?" an IA cop asked me.

"Two, I think," I said. "It happened so quick."

"Break open your weapon."

Doing so, I was amazed to find that I actually had not fired a single round, although I thought I had.

"It happens like that," the detective told me. "In the heat of battle, you're operating off of pure instinct."

As we were returning to our patrol cars, a black man in the crowd jeered at us: "Well, you got your small-arms practice in for today!"

I was still a rook, but his reaction confused me.

What else did this guy think we could have done?

JUST ONE MORE STEP.

It was dawn and I decided I'd stop at my bank after leaving work. I didn't even change out of uniform.

Walking from my personal car, I didn't make it to the front door until I saw the head teller at a window. She was pantomiming not to come in, then pointed at her watch.

Okay, I thought, they're not open yet. I'll drive up the street, buy a paper, and by then I could surely go in and deposit my paycheck.

Returning in ten minutes, I saw two East Point patrol cars parked in the unmistakable position for a felony-in-progress call.

Curious as hell, I entered the bank. The head teller, a chubby woman I went to high school with, came running to me sobbing. "When you came here earlier," she exclaimed through her tears, "there was a man in here with a gun robbing the bank. He saw you and thought we hit the silent alarm. I told him we didn't, that you're just a customer. So he told me if I didn't get rid of you that he was going to shoot you when you came in!"

My blood suddenly turned into ice water.

LAST THOUGHT.

"Mama," the black, teenage boy moaned.

His eyes glazed over as he stared into infinity, lying on his back on a sidewalk only a few blocks from Georgia Baptist Hospital.

The EMTs couldn't save him from all the blood

he'd lost from the bullet wound that entered his back and blasted out from his chest.

He wasn't the first such victim I had to watch die who cried out for their mother at the very end., I reflected as I walked away from that night tableau lit by red lights and blue lights flashing.

Within minutes we had run down his teenaged assassin.

Looking into his cold, hostile eyes, I thought perhaps I could touch some bit of humanity still in him. I said to the boy: "He died calling for his mother."

"He a pussy," he said, his face screwed-up in contempt. As we took him to my patrol car, he didn't struggle against the handcuffs that bound his arms behind his back.

HERE'S LOOKING AT YOU.

"You've done a good job riding herd on the pimps and whores on the Strip," my curly-haired sarge told me. He had radioed for me to five-nine with him on my beat. "I recommended to the major that you work the FIT team. You start tomorrow."

"Thanks, Sarge. I'll do a good job." The Field Investigations Team was a plainclothes assignment in the zone. It wasn't Downtown detectives, but it was a start. I was thrilled. I was twenty-three years-old.

As the sarge drove away beneath the Peachtree Street lights, our dispatcher notified me that Fulton County PD needed an APD patrol car to meet them at the city limits.

Blue lights and siren blazing, I drove my patrol car north, wondering why it was a code 3. It wasn't a help call.

Pulling next to the county unit, I switched off

my lights and siren. "What's the rush?" I asked.

"This," he said, handing a plastic container to me through his window. Curious, I took it, feeling its icy-coldness in my palms. I sat it on the seat next to me, scrutinizing the parcel with my dome light.

"What is it?"

"Eye balls," the other cop said.

"No!" I exclaimed, turning to look at him, thinking he was kidding me because I was a rook.

"I'm serious. It's just been taken from a donor who died and it's needed right away at Crawford Long Hospital for an emergency operation. They need it ASAP."

That sobered me. As I drove Code 3 through the midnight streets of Atlanta, blue lights flashing and siren yelping, I kept my right hand on the precious cargo the whole way.

DETECTIVE DAYS.

LABOR DISPUTE.

I was listening to the Police song on my ghetto blaster: "Roxanne, you don't have to put on the red light" when the armed-robbery-in-progress call crackled over my Zone 2 radio. I was driving my unmarked sedan past the very location.

"I'm twenty-six at that location now, Radio!" I reported in, skidding to a halt and jumping out. "Notify responding units I'm in plainclothes."

This being the busy Peachtree Street Strip, I knew uniform backup would only be seconds away.

It was another call to the Intimo, the sleazy nude bar.

Cautiously ducking my head in the front door, I

saw a huge, naked, black woman with pendulous breasts, swaying on the stage. I recognized her as Peaches. Everything seemed in order in the dive, so I stepped in.

Seeing me, Peaches called out from the stage: "There's a pimp with a knife in the alley, Officer Cartwright!"

Hurrying out the back door, I saw a black man with a knife in his hand apparently about to stab a black female.

"Po-lice! Freeze!" I exclaimed, realizing in an instant that the only way I could stop his knife thrust was to shoot him.

My Smith & Wesson .38 snubnose was in an inside-the-trouser holster. As I leveled the gun on the pimp, the holster was still swaddling my weapon.

I jerked the holster free, but before I could fire a round, the pimp dropped the knife.

Quickly cuffing him, just as the first uniform bound into the alley, the pimp exclaimed: "It ain't what you think! This be my old lady! She kept some money from me an' I was just teachin' her a lesson! I wasn't gonna *really* cut her, man!"

The hooker, wearing a black top so tight it pushed up her brown breasts, said: "He wasn't really gonna cut me. Honest!"

"Do you want to prosecute him for assaulting you?" I asked, although I already anticipated her answer.

"No. He my man."

The best I could do, then, was arrest him for a VKO -- violation of the city's knife ordinance.

As I leaned down to retrieve my holster, the pimp's widening eyes looked at the black snubnose that now dangled at my side.

His knees suddenly buckled beneath him as he slipped to the grimy pavement. "I almost got *shot!* All 'cause of a ho'! It ain't worth it, man! You knew I was just jivin' her, right? You wouldn't of shot me, man. Right?"

Tucking my revolver and holster back into my pants, I didn't admit it, but I was glad I hadn't fired.

Fate is strange sometimes.

VALLEY OF TINY LIGHTS.

An armed robbery call had just come up within the leafy confines of Piedmont Park in Midtown.

Only blocks away, I sped my unmarked Pontiac toward the large park.

"Witnesses just reported a black male armed with a handgun, fitting the perp's seventy-eight, running toward the trail behind the stables," the dispatcher reported.

"Two-twenty-two," I radioed back, "I'm about three seconds from there. Advise units I'm in plainclothes."

Skidding to a halt at the edge of the forest, I

slapped off my headlights, grabbed my flashlight from the seat and leapt from the car. A couple yelled to me: "He just ran down this trail!"

A Mounted Patrol officer came galloping up and dismounted. Our .38s drawn, we cautiously entered the trail.

"He could be hiding in the trees," the officer said as we cut the darkness with our shafts of light.

"Or he could be trying to run through the trail and get onto a street," I countered.

The trail wound down a hill and the pines and oaks cut off the lamp light from the park roads. We were descending into total darkness.

My eyes adjusting to the dark, my skin sweating in the summer heat, I wondered if the armed robber was taking a bead on us as we searched for him.

Then the trail leveled out and I froze. The woods were full of thousands of fireflies. A swirling blizzard of lightning bugs.

"Freeze, motherfucker!" the officer exclaimed,

jarring me from my reverie. He had the perp covered where he lay hiding in a patch of ivy.

As I covered the perp with my .38, the Mounted officer holstered his weapon and quickly fell on the prisoner to hold him down while handcuffing him.

As we ascended the trail, the electric light from the street lamps began washing out the tiny lights of the countless fireflies. Out of the woods, feeling pavement once again beneath my shoes, I saw that more cops were arriving. I felt as though I were emerging from a dream world, hidden away from the harsh reality of the real world.

That incident triggered within me what Zen mystics call *satori*, and Christians an epiphany, a sudden insight. I felt a correlation with my great-Uncle Charlie wearing a rose every day on his beat. There are the ugliness and violence that cops habitually see, contrasted by the simple beauty of a rose, or the sight of countless fireflies floating in the summer air.

Slamming the paddy wagon door behind our perp, I turned and looked at the dark woods before driving out of Piedmont Park.

UNCLE CHARLIE.

The prisoner, a crackhead whose hands we'd cuffed behind his back, was yelling obscenities as I pushed his butt onto the long bench in the basement of police headquarters.

That ugly brown bench has had a million people sit on it, I suddenly realized. Maybe including my great-Uncle Charlie who was hired back in 1929.

He'd pulled the pin after some forty years as a city cop. When I was a kid, Uncle Charlie would pick me up in his white Cadillac. I recall the first time I saw a holstered black pistol strapped to his steering column.

"Is that a *gun?*" I, then a fat eight-year-old,

asked with eyes wide.

"Yep. I used to be a poelease."

"Golly! I wanna be one, too. When I grow up."

"My brother was an officer, too. So was my cousin Glen Pollard. Glen rode a motorcycle."

"You ever *shoot* anybody, Uncle Charlie?" I would later find that all civilians ask this. It's one reason cops socialize with other cops, to avoid this stupid but inevitable question.

"Nope. I never did, but Glen did."

"Did he *kill* the man, Uncle Charlie?"

"Yep. But he didn't feel good about it, Stevie. It's bothered him all his life. But the man would've killed *him*."

Turning up his steep driveway, he drove into the wooded lot where he lived with Aunt Lula in a modest, white-wood house in southwest Atlanta. "You see my picture window there in our living room? People on my beat gave that to me free when I told 'em I was building a house. Poeleases didn't make much pay. Still don't, but it's a good feeling to know you've helped someone who needs it."

As he snipped weeds in his rose garden in the summer sun, I tagged along, asking more questions. "I worked a footbeat Downtown for years and years, on Peters Street," he said, a white straw hat shading his old face. "Used to snip a rose from this garden, like this white rose right here, and wear it stuck in the pocket below my silver badge."

But I didn't want to hear about roses. I wanted to hear about guns and sirens and chases.

Uncle Charlie, in his seventies then, was bald and frail and his smile flickered with the palsy of Parkinson's disease. He would never talk about those kinds of unpleasant things. He went to his grave never telling me the interesting stories I'm sure he knew from experience.

However, he did tell me about the long brown bench in the basement of police headquarters.

"When I got out of the Marines, in 1928, I joined the Atlanta poelease. In those days you didn't get hired right-off. You had to join what they called the soup line. The real name for it was the supernumeraries. The shifts ran twelve hours, and us officers would have to come in for every shift, in full uniform, and sit on this long brown bench in the basement. If a regular officer didn't show up for work, a soup got to take his place for that shift. If every regular poelease showed up, the soup left. Didn't get paid, neither.

"After two years I got hired-on regular. We worked every day with one day off a month. Pay was a hundred bucks a month. Back then you were glad to get it."

"I wanna be a police officer when I grow up."

"I thought you wanted to be a writer."

"Well," I said, frowning. "Maybe I'll be both."

All I can remember seeing then was the top of his straw hat, round and white, as he snipped more weeds from his rose garden.

SHOTS FIRED.

Gene Lassiter, my FIT team partner in 1980, was working an extra job in uniform, so he was going to be late today.

That was okay with me. It was an unseasonably hot Saturday in September. The sun through the windshield of my unmarked police car made me feel languid, as did passing all the al fresco bars on the northside where patrons sat drinking and laughing.

When a patrolman radioed me to five-nine with him at the U.S. Discount gas station across the street from Manuel's Tavern on North Highland Avenue, I was in no rush to get there. Didn't sound drastically important.

Waiting for me was Officer Doug Streval and a tall white-haired man and a gorgeous blonde in a short skirt. "This is the owner of the gas station," said Streval. Seeing my eyes flicker over the blonde, Doug added: "And his secretary. They called because of a suspicious van.

"The manager here went to the C&S bank to drop off a load of money, but saw someone had vandalized the deposit box."

"He couldn't make the drop," the owner interjected. "This is the bank we always use to make the drop. Since he couldn't use this one, he knew he'd have to go to the next C&S, up on Moreland Avenue. But when he started that way, he noticed a van with two black males inside seemed to be following him. So he came back to the station and called me at home."

"The owner wants a cop to ride with them in case of trouble," Doug said. "I figure it'd be better if a plainclothes cop does it. That's why I called you."

"My car is that bomb there," I told the owner apologetically. "As you can see, it's obviously an unmarked police car."

"You can ride in my van," the owner suggested.

"We'll follow my manager who's in his own car."

His secretary smiled when I looked at her, and I suddenly realized I'd volunteer for any detail just to be in her presence -- even riding shotgun on this money drop. Probably wouldn't amount to anything, anyway, but perhaps I might get her number. If I casually mention to her that I frequent Manuel's, she might say: "Oh. I'd really *love* to meet you there sometime."

Almost before I knew it, I was in the van as the owner drove behind his manager. I sat in the back seat, the secretary sat in the passenger seat, speaking in a southern lilt found mostly outside the metro area.

She told me her name. Told me she lived outside the city. Told me where the corporate office was located --

"Look!" exclaimed the owner. "There's a man with a shotgun!"

I was jolted back to reality. He had driven around the rear of the closed bank while his manager had entered through the front. The terrain here was just right for a robbery. The bank sat at the bottom of a hill, concealed from busy Moreland Avenue. Looking through the windshield, I indeed saw a black male rushing through the bushes toward the deposit drop, clutching a shotgun.

As I leaped from the van, pulling my .38 with my right hand and clasping my walkie-talkie in my left, I saw the perp jut the sawed-off shotgun at the manager, who dropped the money bag.

Suddenly time was going in slow motion. "Freeze, motherfucker!" I shouted as I saw him swing his shotgun around my way. The realization that he was about to blast my body in half made me tighten the grip on my radio: I didn't want to lose that, I would have to call for an ambulance for myself once the blast knocked me to the ground.

BLAM! BLAM! BLAM! BLAM! BLAM! I'm firing my weapon at the perp, hoping I'm hitting him before he can hit me, the smell of cordite biting my nostrils like fire ants.

He dropped the shotgun and ran, and I think I'm not hit, wonder if he even got off a round or not.

Then time returned to normal. I wasn't hurt and the manager was cowering for cover, and the perp gone. Running up the steep hill, traffic was zipping along, but I didn't see the armed robber. A man, walking a dog on a leash, approached. "Did you see a black male just run up this hill?"

"Wearing a red-spotted shirt? Sure did. He just ran that way."

"*Fifty-nine right away!*" I radioed. "*Shots fired!*"

Almost immediately distant sirens exploded all around.

Within minutes, a rookie pulled the perp from under a parked car only a block away. I shot five rounds, only one hit him. In the arm. It was so quick -- yet so slow in my mind.

Turned out he was an old-time armed robber, first convicted when I was two- years old.

I never saw the sexy secretary again, but the owner gave me permission to park on his lot for all of eternity. It being across from Manuel's, I was grateful.

DESCENT INTO THE UNDERWORLD.

I was a Zone 2 Field Investigator when I made my descent into the underworld.

The MARTA underground line was being dug that summer. This evening was hot summer and I wore a black tee shirt with my jeans.

I spotted a felon I had a warrant for, strolling down Peachtree Street, and as soon as he saw my unmarked detective car heading his way, he put it in the wind.

"Unit two-twenty-two in pursuit of a felony suspect!" I radioed as my adrenaline kicked in to high gear. He ran through where they were constructing the MARTA Midtown station and I had to jump out after him. He ran into the huge construction hole, lit sparingly with flood lights, and as we descended into the earth, I could no longer hear the sirens of my approaching backup units, nor would my police radio transmit or receive.

I slipped and slid in the mud, as no concrete had yet been poured there, and the air turned frigid at that low level and I could see my breaths.

I was tired, but the perp was more tired, and I caught and cuffed him. Back on the surface of the world, it was torrid hot and the Midtown night pulsed with a dozen flashing blue lights.

"YOU MAY THINK I'M SOME KINDA NUT."

In 1979, some mothers, whose children had recently been slain, made public their suspicions that a serial killer was targeting poor children in Atlanta. Responding to this, the administration created a Task Force and assigned detectives to it.

Two FIT officers from all of the then-five patrol zones were to assist the Task Force one day a week. Mostly we were given names phoned in anonymously (and there must have been thousands) and we investigated them. These were the less-likely suspects, as the Homicide Task force detectives Downtown were pursuing the better leads, but the city wanted no stone left unturned.

I received a very mysterious phone call from New Orleans, Louisiana, one afternoon in 1980. It was a deep-voiced white man in a motel room who said he was a traveling salesman. "You may think I'm some kinda nut, but I'm definitely not, so please hear me out."

"Okay. I'm listening."

"I'm in New Orleans on business and I saw on the news about the missing and murdered kids in Atlanta. I went to sleep last night and had a psychic dream about who might be the killer. The message was to tell my information to `a Detective Cartwright in Atlanta.' I've never been to Atlanta and I don't know anyone there, including you, but I get psychic flashes from time to time."

Despite my skepticism, I wrote down everything he told me. This, after all, could be the paranormal Truth my soul sought. Several other clairvoyants had come to Atlanta to also offer their services. I, the Wolf Shaman who thinks Uncle Charlie's ghost opens elevators for me, am not a strict disbeliever in the supernatural as my newspaper days will attest. But, as a detective, I also knew that the killer could be one of these so-called psychics and in that way they might feed us real information about their crimes. As a cop I'd learned that a lead sometimes comes to us in bizarre ways. So I encouraged the man to continue with his story, and I assured him, "I'm not scoffing at your professed powers, believe me."

"I was skeptical about my dream," he resumed,

"then I turned on the TV set in my motel room and the old show *Bonanza* was on. You're familiar with that show, right?"

"I've been called Hoss and Little Joe a hundred times."

"Well, that struck me as a sign, but I still wasn't totally convinced until I jumped to my feet to look out the window. And there in the parking lot was a truck with the words `Ponderosa Ice Cream.' That compelled me to make a long-distance phone call to Atlanta and inquire if there was a Detective Cartwright working on the missing and murdered children. The operator told me there was and I requested they have you call me. Do you believe me, Detective Cartwright?"

"I'm taking notes, sir. Who do you think our killer is?"

"The dream revealed to me that it's a Satanic cult. They're using the kidnapped kids as human sacrifices. In the dream I saw black candles and unholy emblems and bloody altars."

As it turned out, the mysterious caller was wrong. It was a local freelance photographer named Wayne Williams. My theory is that there were no serial killings until the mothers went public. The investigations tend to show the early cases were not related. Williams, who fit the profile of a serial killer, was above average intelligence, and I think he became the killer after the mothers had generated the possibly spurious publicity.

Williams was arrested, tried and convicted in 1982 of two of the murders.

ROBBERY STAKEOUT.

Anything can happen in a stakeout. It's sometimes fraught with irony. When a violent crime goes down, the stakeout cops have to take care of business in a way that won't endanger innocent civilians. Sometimes Fate throws us a sucker punch.

The January 1981, night was frigid. Working in blue jeans and a heavy coat, I felt so insulated that I doubted I could move easily if I had to struggle with a perp.

My partner, Larry Chappell, who still retained his Marine buzzcut, held a shotgun in his hands. We sat in our unmarked car on a side street down from the dumpy redneck bar we were staking out.

Officers Billy "Too Tall" King and Steve Walden, in uniform, were hiding among some trees across the street from the Austin Avenue Buffet. The oddly named tavern was supposed to be robbed tonight, based on information given to a Narcotics detective from one of his snitches. From King and Walden's vantage point, they could see directly into the small bar through the storefront.

When these two notified us the robbery was going down, all units were to would converge on the bar. We had already agreed that, to not put the patrons in jeopardy, we would snatch the perp after he fled the bar. The snitch said the perp would be on foot, as he owned no car and all money he got went to buy dilaudid.

"What time is it?" Chappell asked.

Checking my luminous wristwatch, I said: "About ten minutes till closing time."

"Looks like it's not goin' down tonight." We'd already been waiting almost two hours. That made me think of a stakeout axiom popular with cops: Stakeouts are hours and hours of boredom often interrupted by moments of sheer terror.

Rubbing my hands together for heat, I was just as glad if it wouldn't go down. "Hell," I told Chappell. "I think my trigger finger's frozen, anyway."

Then Walden's voice crackled over our handie-talkie: "Get ready. Looks like it's going down."

I turned off the engine and Chappell and I waited to hear further from Walden.

"It's going down," Walden radioed, the excitement audible in his voice. "He's still inside.

Move into position. OK! He's coming out! He's coming out!"

We bolted from the car and ran toward the bar a block away, Chappell racking a live round into the chamber of his shotgun.

Still running, I saw a yellow cab zip to a stop in front of the bar.

"What's *this?*" I exclaimed, watching the perp run from the bar and open the back door of the cab.

"Too Tall" King, 5'5", and the 6'4" Walden were running to it from across the street, .38s drawn, as Chappell and I hurried in from our side.

"Police! Freeze! Don't move!" we were yelling. "Hands in the air! Hands in the air!"

Chappell had his shotgun pointed at the perp who nonetheless threw himself into the back of the cab. All our guns were on him. I could see the cabbie then. She was a female so fat that her belly wedged her under the steering wheel. Seeing all the guns pointing at her cab, she became hysterical, but her flab jammed her so that she could not hide.

"Throw your gun out!" we yelled.

"I ain't got no gun," said the blond-haired perp. "What gun?"

"Put your hands up where we can see them!"

Slowly, he complied. I saw no gun.

We yanked him from the cab and cuffed his hands behind his back. He had a slack-mouthed face with empty eyes and stringy, straw-colored hair. He didn't look like a rocket scientist. "I ain't got no gun. I ain't done nothin'."

"Here it is," Walden said, retrieving an H&R six-shot revolver from the shadows of the back seat.

Searching the perp, his pockets were stuffed with the $3,162 he'd just robbed from the bar and its few patrons.

"You ain't done nothin', huh?" I jeered at him.

"Hey, I seen it go down, but I didn't do it!"

"We were watching you from across the street," Walden told him, as the patrons scurried from the bar pointing at the perp.

It seemed that the cabbie was in with the

robber.

I tried to speak to her, but she was crying hysterically, ranting into her microphone to her dispatcher.

"Do we take her in, too?" Chappell asked.

"She *must* be his getaway," I said. "How else could she so conveniently arrive just as the perp's fleeing the bar?"

"Oh, no, that's my cab," one of the patrons slurred. "I'm too drunk ta walk home, so I had the bartender call me a cab."

Skeptical, I looked at the bartender, still shaking from having a gun stuck in his face. "Is that true?"

"Y-Yes, sir. I called the cab for Louie here."

"Then we probably better try to calm her down before she gives herself a heart attack."

As we escorted the failed robber to an awaiting squad car, I muttered to Chappell: "This is the damned craziest stakeout I've *ever* been on."

Chappell chuckled.

YOU DON'T PAY HER.

Cindy volunteered to act as bait to catch the rapist.

Looking at the zone cop's girlfriend, a buxom brunette, the word "Entrapment" flashed like a blue light in my head.

"This could be *dangerous,* Cindy," protested Billy "Too Tall" King, her short but handsome boyfriend. He and Cindy looked cute together.

"The plan," I interjected, "is for Cindy to call the cab company my perp works for. Have her tell them she has a special for Ned."

"What's a `special'?" Billy asked suspiciously.

"It's cabbie lingo meaning the patron requests a specific driver."

"I'm special," cooed Cindy playfully and I tried to repress the fantasy playing in my own head.

"When Ned hears a lone female is giving him a special," I said, "he'll be so turned on he'll have tunnel vision. You and me will be waiting in the shopping center parking lot, Billy. Cindy'll be standing outside the Waffle House where he can see her from the street. We'll snatch his ass up before he ever gets to Cindy."

"I'll do it," Cindy said, smiling in feigned innocence. I could see Billy gritting his teeth.

By that day, June 29, 1981, I already had a good idea of what made my perp tick. I held rape warrants for the cab driver, but I knew there would be problems in the case. His three victims were hookers. When Brenda, one of my snitches, flagged my unmarked car down on Ponce de Leon Avenue NE and nonchalantly told me she'd been raped, I replied jokingly: "How do you rape a hooker, Brenda? Not pay her?"

"I'm serious, Cartwright," the country girl

countered. Brenda had a slender body with firm breasts. If she wasn't a hooker, she might be attractive. "I know I'm a prostitute an' a junkie, an' all, but he *did* rape me."

"I thought you were joking. Tell me what happened."

It happened two months ago, she told me. The twenty-year-old with slightly cocked eyes was working Ponce when a fiftyish white man with short gray hair and glasses pulled up in a green car.

Brenda slid into the trick's car and he drove to what we then called the state property. It was an entire neighborhood that the state had condemned to construct a road. Neighbors sued to block the project and they tied it up in litigation for years, during which time nature took over where the DOT had razed the houses. It created an unofficial park in the residential area. Winos lived in the thicket. At the time, I drove a Jeep CJ7 and would slip and slide through the rough terrain there. Off-duty, we'd taken some nurses and waitresses, and booze, and had a bonfire under one of the oldest trees in Atlanta. I fondly recalled that my last off-duty visit there. I and a secretary were alone, kissing in my CJ, when a neighbor came by walking his dog.

From that same hill you could see the lights of Downtown to the south. The Northern army used this hill in the civil war to bomb Atlanta. The state would later abandon plans for a road here and the property became the Jimmy Carter Presidential Library. Much history passed over that hallowed ground, including the rape of Brenda the prostitute.

"Once we got there," Brenda told me, "he pulled out a snub-nosed, blue steel thirty-eight an' an icepick. He told me to give him head or he'd kill me. I never expected that from the old guy. If he just wanted to use force 'cause it turned him on, Cartwright, I coulda dealt with that, but I was really afraid he was gonna kill me."

Fellating him in the front seat, once he ejaculated, he tried to blindfold Brenda, but she resisted out of fear he intended to kill her.

Deciding this was life or death, Brenda bolted from the car. She was savvy enough to glimpse the tag, BAA 760, as she fled through the woods to the nearest street.

"Why'd you wait two months to tell us, Brenda?"

"Because I'm a hooker, Cartwright. I figured ya'll won't care. But it ain't right what he done to me. An' he's done it to two other workin' girls."

"Will they give me a statement? Will they prosecute him?"

"They said they would if you'll get the bastard."

****

The tag was registered to N. C. Lansing, 32 Peachtree Avenue in northeast Atlanta, north of Midtown. I drove Brenda there and she spotted the car parked in the apartment complex. It was a green Dodge Dart.

Checking his record in ID, I found Lansing had

priors for sexual crimes. ID listed him as having escaped from a North Carolina prison fifteen years ago. He was serving time for rape. Somehow he had since been arrested and released on bond by APD without the escape warrant being detected. Lansing's priors included rape, peeping tom, burglary, loitering, assault and robbery.

Showing Brenda a photo lineup, she identified Lansing as her attacker.

"Now let's go talk to those other two girls, Brenda. Can you take me to them?"

"Sure. It's fun ridin' in a narc car an' not be goin' to jail!"

Pamela was a short, thin eighteen-year-old with straight, black hair. When we spotted her working Ponce, Brenda leaned out of the car window and called her over. Thin legs protruded from a pair of violet hotpants. I assumed she could remove them quickly when she was with a trick.

"Tell Cartwright what happened to you."

Climbing into the back seat, Pamela lit a

cigarette and gazed out the window. "It was about five in the morning. A green car -- a Dodge Swinger, I think -- stopped and I got in."

"How long ago was this?"

"Yesterday."

"Of course, you didn't make a police report, right?"

"I didn't figger it'd do no good."

"Outcry in rape cases is always a problem. You being hookers is going to make getting an indictment even tougher."

"We got rights, too!" protested Brenda. "It ain't right what he done!"

"Look, I've already said I'm going to do what I can. So, Pamela, you got in the green Dodge with this trick. What did he look like?"

"Chubby, old white guy with glasses. I asked if he wanted a date. He asked how much I wanted for a blow job. I told him thirty dollars and he said he'd give me twenty-five.

"He didn't wanna go to my apartment, he said

he just wanted to park somewhere, so I told him how to get to Phylant Street." That was a cul de sac of businesses next to a railroad track. After hours it was desolate, so the hookers used it. Every morning, at the beginning of the legitimate work day, employees had to walk around oozing rubbers on the pavement.

"He parked behind a building and turned off the engine and pulled a gun from under his seat. He pointed the gun at me and said `Bang, bang.' Then I reached for the door handle on my side and it was gone."

"He learned that from me," Brenda interjected like a helpful child. "Remember, Cartwright, I told you I was able to get out when he tried to blindfold me?"

"I remember, Brenda. Go on, Pamela."

Without emotion, she continued: "He pushed me to the floorboard. He grabbed my head and made me suck his dick. The whole time I was giving him head he had the gun to my head.

"He didn't come, and real soon he kinda got

scared. He said we better go to another place. I told him there wasn't any need to go someplace else, that we should get in the back seat and make love. He let his guard down then and I came up off the floor and kicked him in the balls. I climbed like hell over the back seat and I remember seeing an icepick in his hand."

"Where was the gun you said he had?"

"I don't know. He musta switched it for the icepick. It was dark."

"So you're climbing over the seat to escape."

"And he turned back toward me and says `You want this icepick in your guts?' Then I grabbed his glasses and kept smashin' them against the inside of the car until they was busted. Then I rolled down the back passenger's window and climbed out and ran home."

"Look at these photos, Pamela," I said, handing her the same array of mug shots I had earlier shown Brenda. "Do you see the guy?"

"This is him," she declared, handing me the

photo of Ned Lansing.

****

Brenda had one more hooker to direct me to. Penny was a twenty-four-year-old with coiled brown hair and the forlorn look of a veteran drug addict. Like most street hookers, these three looked sexy -- but on closer inspection you could see that they'd been rode hard and hung up wet. Cops work with a lot of hookers and I knew any of them would give us free☐ sex. But as soon as that happened they'd tell everybody on the street and they would destroy that cop's reputation. The street people would lose all respect for him.

"Penny's story's gonna knock your socks off, Cartwright," Brenda promised with glee, exposing her gap-toothed smile. I was picturing these three on the stand, and it didn't seem promising, but I had promised them I would do something.

After Penny slammed the rear car door and

related her story, it sounded similar to Brenda's and Pamela's. But it was about to get more bizarre.

"This was last December, Cartwright. This white guy in his fifties, wearing glasses and a white cap -- "

"I forgot to tell you about the white cap," interrupted Brenda. "He was wearing it when he did me, too."

"Let her finish her story, Brenda. Penny. Can you describe the car?"

"Kind of a green Dodge Swinger. I think it was a Swinger. He stopped next to a building and said he wanted to fuck. I told him there was too much light here, we could get caught, then he pulls this blue-steel revolver and points it at me. Gimme a smoke, Brenda."

As Brenda pulled a crumpled pack from her dirty jeans, there was silence in the detective car. I noticed Penny wore no bra, and her top was so low-cut that, the way she sat, I could see her brown nipples and a rose tattoo over her heart. After sucking the weed lit, Penny continued in the same detached manner as had Pamela. "He said if I make any noise he'll stab me in the gut with an icepick."

"I thought he had a gun?"

"That's just what he said."

"He's got this hard-on about icepicks," Brenda interjected.

"Next he pulled down the sun visor and I could see a piece of white adhesive tape stuck there. He put it over my eyes so I couldn't see and he pushed me down in the seat and told me not to sit up. When I tried to sit up, he pushed my head back down."

"The bastard *would* have done that to *me!*"

"Let her *talk*, Brenda."

"I started crying and the tape got loose at the bottom. I could see a little then. He drove a long way and stopped. When he stopped he put a coat over my head and took me out of the car. He told me to be careful because we were going up a few steps."

"About what time was this?" I asked.

"Way after midnight. Maybe two. So, he led me

up some steps and I could see a little out the bottom of the tape, remember, and I could see the red brick front of an apartment building." The suspect, I recalled, lived in just such a building. "He took me through one door and then into another door that was his apartment on the first floor.

"When we got inside, he said he wanted to fuck me. He said he uses the gun and the bandages because the girls always rush him. He asked my name and I lied. I think I told him my name was Donna."

Leaving the tape on her eyes, he forced her to strip. Leading her to a bed, he had intercourse with her for only two or three minutes. While the brief coitus took place, Penny was scanning the room through the loose tape. "I saw two metal rolls of adhesive tape on the bedside table."

Tossing her cigarette butt through her open window, she took a deep breath. "When he was through, he told me to get dressed. He gave me two twenty-dollar bills and led me back to his car."

"You're still blindfolded?" I asked.

"Yeah. He didn't take the tape off 'till we were back on Ponce. He helped me out of the car. I tried to get around back to see his tag, but he brought me around the front. I saw a dude I knew, he was across the street, and I screamed for help and ran toward him. I was crying, telling my friend what happened to me. We got in his car and tried to chase the green car down, but he was already gone by then."

"Had you ever dated the guy in the green Dodge before this?"

"No, but I saw him on Ponce about five months later. He was still driving the same car, cruising for a girl. I saw him a month later and memorized his tag."

"Do you still remember it?"

"I sure the hell do. BAA 760."

"Look at these pictures, Penny. Do you see the guy?"

It did not surprise me whose mug shot she handed to me over the car seat.

****

Going alone to the apartment complex, I casually searched the names on the mail boxes. Lansing was listed on the box for apartment number six.

Back at the Zone 2 FIT office, I typed an arrest warrant, listing the three incidents, the tag number two of the victims reported, and the use or threat to use an icepick. I also typed a search warrant for the perp's apartment. A judge signed them. I didn't mention in the warrants that the victims were prostitutes.

Learning that Lansing was a local cabbie, I decided that taking him down at work would be safest, instead of going to his apartment. That was how we recruited Cindy, the Zone 2 cop's girlfriend, to act as bait.

Billy and I would take the perp down in the busy parking lot of the Lindbergh shopping center. Billy was in his marked squad car, I in my unmarked sedan, where we watched Cindy from the length of a football field as she called the cab company from a pay phone. As she waited alone, she stood in a way that made her well-rounded breasts jut forward. I wondered if she designed this to turn-on Billy. It was certainly affecting me.

Within five minutes we saw a cab hurtling our way. "Let's take him down!" Billy exclaimed as Lansing drove into the lot, craning his neck toward the Waffle House. Cindy stood in his path as Billy zipped behind the cab, his blue lights ripping. But Lansing had tunnel vision. He only saw Cindy. Billy turned on the siren, and only then did Lansing look to his rear view mirror. He slowed. Billy almost smacked the bumper of the cab. Finally Lansing stopped, twenty feet from Cindy, and we rushed him.

Pulling Lansing from his cab, I declared: "Ned Lansing, I have a warrant for your arrest for rape. Do you have a gun in your cab?"

"Yes. I'll get it for you," he said with a Tennessee drawl, reaching through his opened door.

"Not a good idea," I said, grabbing his arm and pulling him back to cuff him.

Cindy now had an interesting tale to tell at Manuel's that night.

****

We took Lansing to my office where I Mirandized him. His drug store cologne battled weakly against the smell of fear coming from his underarms. His slightly bucked teeth made Lansing look like a seedy Alvin the chipmunk.

After relating my evidence to him, he admitted he picks up hookers, and shrugged it off.

"Do you also admit to taking prostitutes to your apartment?" I asked.

"Sure. Why not? But I didn't *rape* any of those whores." He looked sneaky, pushing his black frame glasses back up his nose. His pale hand trembled. "How can you rape a *whore,* anyway?"

"You'll take a polygraph, then?"

"No. I won't do that. And I don't want to talk

about any alleged `incidents' because you cops would say that's a confession. And that won't help me."

"Okay. Let's talk about your escape from prison fifteen years ago. You're still wanted for that."

"The FBI picked me up for that years ago but North Carolina didn't want to extradite. They let me go."

"I don't know about that, but they say they'll extradite now."

Before tallying up all his charges, we executed a search warrant at his apartment. Besides the adhesive tape rolls Penny had spotted on his bedside table, I confiscated two icepicks, another adhesive tape roll, a twenty-two-calibre rifle in his closet, a brown sack containing ten plastic bags of marijuana, and four joints in a tin can on a living room table. In two photo albums were nude photos of prostitutes and sexy young ladies who looked as though they were professional strippers. Most photos were of them in bed, legs spread for Lansing's camera.

"What the hell is *this?*" I exclaimed after pulling his headboard from the wall. "It's some kind of cord." Billy walked over and helped me pull the entire bed from the wall. "It's a microphone!" Lansing had a microphone taped to the back of his headboard. Following the cord, it led to a tape recorder in the bedside table drawer. Next to it were eight cassette tapes. "I wonder what the hell *this* is?" I muttered, confiscating the tapes.

****

At my office, I listened to the first cassette. Getting on the phone, I called Detective Ford in Sex Crimes. "Bobby, you gotta come down here and listen to this tape!"

After Ford and I listened, it was obvious. "He's recording himself having sex with prostitutes," said Ford. At the end of each tape we could hear him thanking her and counting out her pay.

But one tape wasn't so polite. The voice

sounded like a very young woman, maybe a teenager. "Don't hit me again, please," she pleaded. At another point she implores: "Please take this tape off my eyes. I won't tell on you, honest." There's a sound like a slap and the girl whimpers.

Returning to the jail, I wasn't surprised when Lansing refused to talk about the girl on the tape.

By this time I had eleven felony charges against him: rape, three counts of aggravated sodomy, three aggravated assaults, pointing a pistol at another, convicted felon in possession of a firearm, possession of marijuana, and kidnapping. The three hookers were the main victims.

The city solicitor preparing for the prelim was shocked when I told him the victims were prostitutes. He didn't want to proceed but I insisted. Brenda, Pamela, and Penny testified, dressed more like coeds than hookers, and Lansing was bound-over for possible grand jury indictment.

Meanwhile I tried to learn the identity of the one girl on the tape. I let hookers hear it to see if they recognized her, but none did. I checked with Homicide to see if they had any found bodies that might be her. Still, no leads. Checking with Missing Persons, they had hundreds of reported runaways that *could* be the girl. I have never identified her. Could it have just been a sex game? If it was, they should nominate her for an Oscar. She sounded terrified and in pain.

****

The Fulton County DA's office would not indict someone for raping a hooker. I went to the New Indictments section to plead my case, telling the ADA about the tape with the terrified girl.

"This perp is dangerous," I said. "He uses a gun and an icepick, and tapes the victim's eyes."

"But they're *hookers*. We'd never find a jury to convict."

"What if he killed that girl on the tape? What if her body's lying buried somewhere?"

"So get some evidence and charge him with murder."

"I'm going to bring you that tape and let you listen to it. You decide then."

The ADA arranged a special plea bargain for Lansing. Not presented to the grand jury for indictment were: convicted felon in possession of a firearm, two counts of aggravated sodomy, one count of kidnapping, pointing a pistol at another, two counts of rape, and possession of marijuana with intent to distribute.

As part of the plea, Lansing agreed to plead guilty to one count of kidnapping; the ADA downgraded one aggravated assault to simple battery, and one pointing a pistol he downgraded to simple battery. The judge sentenced Lansing to serve one year in prison, then to be extradited to North Carolina, where he had escaped from prison, to serve the remaining fifteen years of his sentence for rape.

The sentence satisfied the three victims more

than it did me. Brenda continued her trade and her lifestyle until a cop found her dead on the street from a drug overdose. The other two hookers seem to have just faded away. Maybe they've gone straight and are raising a family. (Don't bet on it.) After I retired from APD, I became very active in dog Rescue (that's another book); my first group held dog adoptions at a PetSmart built on my old beat on Ponce de Leon Ave NE. One of the hookers got too old to work the street and got a job there. When she saw me working with the Rescue dogs, she proudly told me she had kicked street life and drugs and entered what they call the straight life. Few street people are so lucky.

A SLIME OF PASSION.

When you're executing a search warrant for a

live snake, you open all drawers with extreme caution.

What led me to this search was an incident on September 17, 1981, at the Siam Zoo pet store on Cheshire Bridge Road in northeast Atlanta.

Two white guys in their early twenties, one a sandy blond with a small mustache, and the other a darker blond with no facial hair, entered the store. When Jan, an employee, asked if she could help them, the one with the mustache replied, "I called earlier about a boa constrictor."

"That would be the Bolivian red-tail," Jan said. "Would you like to see it?"

"Yes," said the mustached one. "I'd like to hold it."

Going to the terrarium, Jan bravely reached in and removed the coiling, three-foot- long serpent. The guys' eyes seemed to glow when they held the snake.

"How much do you want for it?"

"This baby boa sells for two-hundred-and-fifty

dollars."

"Okay," the mustached one said cautiously. "Do you have a used tank we could buy? To put the boa into?"

"I'll have to check with the owner, Doctor Putnam," she said. "He's in the back."

Returning to tell them the price of the vivarium, Jan saw the two guys *and* the boa constrictor were gone.

This wasn't the only theft I'd ever worked at the exotic pet store. I had arrested a burglar for stealing an expensive Macaw only months ago, so I thought my luck was good with the Siam.

When I entered, Suzy, a huge, pet chimp, sat on a high stool smoking a cigarette. She ignored me.

Dave Putnam, the store owner, was also a clinical psychologist. When he came to me from his back office, I asked him what sort of psychological profile he would make for someone who would steal a snake.

Firing up a cigarette as he thought, the wiry,

thirtyish man with a shock of black hair, responded: "I'd say they're lacking in social skills. A loner, probably not someone popular with girls. They may tend to identify with the cold cunning of a snake."

Luckily, I also had more tangible leads to work.

"I recall someone calling about the price of that particular snake," Putnam told me, blowing a plume of cigarette smoke. "He said his name was John and he left a call-back number."

"Do you still have the number?"

"I wrote it down somewhere," he said quickly, stubbing his cigarette out in an overflowing ashtray near the cash register. "Let me search for it."

I left Siam Zoo with my first lead. Now I needed to trace the number.

****

On September 22, I served a Subpoena for the Production of Documents to the security division of Southern Bell.

"This is a new number," the security rep told me, checking her screen. "It's not yet on our computers." Clacking her fingernails over the keyboard, she added: "It appears to have been installed on the seventeenth."

That was the very date of the theft.

The record check showed Southern Bell listed the new phone line to Michael Hutson in Clarkston, a metro Atlanta town.

Hutson was not to be found in APD's criminal history files, so I tried Dekalb County. They'd arrested him earlier that year for shoplifting.

Driving to Dekalb Police Headquarters, a Records clerk handed me Hutson's mug shot. At the time of his shoplifting arrest, he listed his occupation as an x-ray technician for a small, metro hospital. Seeing he was single reminded me of Dr. Putnam's impromptu psychological profile of a "loner."

****

Making a photo lineup of five white males, I slid the mug shot of Hutson into the stack and drove back to the Siam Zoo.

Taking Jan to the side, I handed her the color photos.

Scrutinizing the photos, she said: "This is one of them." She held the photo of Michael Hutson. "He was the one with the mustache, the one who seemed to be the leader -- so to speak."

Away from Jan, I showed the photos to another employee who recalled seeing the two guys loitering in the store for about an hour on the date of the theft.

She, too, identified Hutson's mug shot.

****

What I really needed now was to recover the stolen snake.

Although I secured an arrest warrant for Hutson, based on his being identified in the photo lineup by the two employees, tangible evidence would help. Plus, Dr. Putnam wanted his snake returned.

The only way to recover the boa was to get a search warrant for the suspect's apartment. It being outside my jurisdiction, I couldn't go about securing the warrant in the usual way.

Knowing a superior court judge has statewide powers, and our municipal court judges do not, I went to the Fulton County Superior Court. There a judge signed the warrant allowing me to search the Clarkston apartment.

****

On the twenty-first, I had my dispatcher call Dekalb PD and request officers meet me to execute the search warrant.

The first officer arrived, a lanky young man with red hair. "What are we searching for?" he asked. "Drugs?"

"No," I said. "A snake."

"You're kidding -- right?"

"No. It's a boa constrictor." After I explained the case to him, I noticed his face blanched.

"Hey," he finally protested, "*I'm* not getting bit by some snake!"

"Boas don't bite," I told him. "They kill their prey by constriction. Besides, I'm told this is just a baby boa."

"Yeah?" he asked suspiciously. "And just how *long* is this baby snake?"

"Three feet."

None of the uniforms were happy about this, and they talked it over among themselves. It made matters worse, no doubt, that I was a detective from another jurisdiction asking them to assist on this unusual search warrant.

"We'll go with you," the redhead finally told me. "But we'll just be there for backup. *You* get to search for the damn snake."

I wasn't enthused, but, after all, it *was* my

warrant.

****

The young man who opened the door was not Hutson, but he resembled the second suspect. The one I had not yet identified.

"What's the problem, officers?" he asked.

With the Dekalb uniforms behind me, I handed the man a copy of the court document. "I have a search warrant for this apartment," I said as our entourage walked past the dumbfounded guy. "Is Michael Hutson here?"

"He lives here. He's my roommate. But he isn't home right now."

"What's your name?"

"John Ponder."

That rang a bell. The caller to the Siam, before the theft, had said he was looking for a baby boa and that his name was "John." Here, no doubt, was my other perp.

True to their word, the Dekalb cops watched as I *carefully* opened every drawer and cabinet in the clean, middle-income apartment. Although I knew boas don't bite, every drawer I opened gave me visions of some demonic viper leaping out at me, burying its fangs deep into my brain.

"Where's the damn snake?" I demanded to John after searching the entire place.

"I don't know anything about a snake," he said, but he could not look me in the eyes.

"Have you ever been arrested before, John?"

"I've got some traffic tickets -- "

"What we're talking about here, John, is a *felony*. You guys may think it was cute to heist that snake -- but you guys are going to jail over this. You can go to prison. How long do you think a guy like you would last with a bunch of hardened convicts?"

He began fidgeting, looking like a trapped rabbit. "I've never even been to any pet store on Cheshire Bridge," he said, his voice faltering.

"Okay, John, play dumb, but you're in over

your head here. The best thing you and Michael can do is return the snake in good shape and hope that'll appease the judge some."

****

I had hardly gotten back to my office in the Zone 2 precinct when my phone rang.

"This is Mike Hutson," an unsure voice said. "My roommate told me you have a warrant or something for me."

"I do, Mike. And I want that snake returned to the Siam Zoo. I'm in the process of also getting an arrest warrant for your roommate. I suggest, Mike, that you two turn yourselves in."

Within two hours, the two young men, who were only a few years younger than me, sat before my desk, their heads hung low.

After Mirandizing them, I asked: "Now where is the damn snake?"

They declined to make statements until conferring with their attorney.

While awaiting the wagon that would transport them to city jail, Hutson asked: "If we and the Siam Zoo come to an agreement, would you drop the theft charge?"

"That's impossible. Return of the snake would probably help your sentencing. It might be the difference between jail time and probation."

"I'm *already* on probation for theft," Hutson muttered, looking disgusted.

Dr. Putnam had already called and told me Hutson called him, offering a hundred dollars and the return of the boa constrictor if Putnam would drop charges. "I told them to call *you,*" Putnam had told me.

****

A week later, after this duo had been bound-over to the grand jury for indictment, Floyd Barnett, an employee of Siam called me.

"A man just came into the store," he said. "He

told me he was returning the snake to its lawful owner."

"What condition is the boa in?"

"Bad, but it'll live. The man said he was John's father. I gave him a receipt for the snake. Doctor Putnam wants to know if you'll need to retain the boa for evidence?"

Chuckling, I said: "I don't think APD has the facilities to house a snake. You keep it."

This wasn't the last incident APD had with the Siam Zoo. Dr. Putnam took Suzy, his large, pet chimp, to a yuppie bar near his shop, where she was a great conversation piece as he and she sat at a table drinking beer.

On one such visit, Suzy must have imbibed too much. She went tearing out of the bar, chased by Putnam. She terrorized busy Piedmont Road. After she chased a doughnut shop waitress, someone called APD.

None of the cops had ever handled a rampaging, drunken ape call before. After she bit a wrecker driver, it became serious.

An officer ended up shooting and killing Suzy.

I saw Dr. Putnam right after that. He was in the back of a Zone 2 car, weeping pitifully for his dead friend.

It wasn't much later that he sold the Siam Zoo and I have never heard from him again. I guess he was in mourning for Suzy.

****

I spent five years working FIT. Other cops can have their UC assignments, or stakeout, or uniform patrol, detective work was what I had always aspired to. In 1983 the chief promoted me to criminal investigator. Hello, Vice squad. Goodbye, good ole Zone 2.

LISTENER SANDWICH.

Our sergeant, a black man so big we called him Oak Tree, came upon an inspired idea. "We'll hit liquor houses on Friday and Saturday night," he told all of us assigned to the Vice squad. Liquor houses were speakeasies in several lower-class black neighborhoods. Here I sniffed the noxious fumes of my first "listener sandwich." It was a pot of pig ears boiling on a stove to be eaten between two pieces of bread as the patrons purchased bottled beer or liquor by the shot, and gambled.

Raids at these places usually yielded thirty or more arrests at a time. The way we did it, a black Vice detective gained entry to the residential house where illegal activity was known to go on. We'd give him about ten minutes, after which, if he hadn't come back outside, we realized he would have purchased a drink and seen the illegal activity taking place. These were all city ordinance violations, not even state misdemeanors.

We'd rush in, taking care of business, screaming "Poe - lease! Poe - lease!" never knowing in advance if this was a small group or if we were to be outnumbered. Some patrons in these liquor houses were nonviolent, often elderly people just looking for a place in the neighborhood to socialize and get a drink. But desperadoes also frequented these joints. It wasn't uncommon to raid a place, yelling for everybody in the usually dark houses to grab the wall, while hearing the usual thunks and thuds of knives and even pistols dropped by perps before we had a chance to search for them.

"This isn't the kind of detective work I'm interested in," I told the sarge after a few weeks. He stood a good foot taller than me.

"But the chief wants all new detectives in CID to work Vice for a minute."

"I worked vice cases on the FIT team. This is wasting my potential, Sarge."

"Just hang in there, Cartwright. It'll be over

before you know it."

MUDDY THE WATERS.

I arrested a hooker for propositioning me.

Her attorney drove himself into municipal court in a motorized wheelchair. I felt sorry for Stanley, but despite his disability he had a large clientele. Most of them were hookers, like this sad-eyed drug addict I was testifying against.

"I was working an undercover vice detail, your honor, and in that capacity I noticed the defendant flagging cars at the corner of Fifth and Piedmont. She flagged me down and came to my van when I stopped.

"She asked me if I was a cop, and I said I

wasn't. She then told me she would give me a blowjob for fifteen dollars. At that point I arrested her for prostitution."

Her lawyer then had an opportunity to cross examine me.

"Detective, did you ask my client what her profession was?"

I had to grin, as did the judge. "It was apparent, Counselor, what line of work the defendant is in." The court room audience chuckled and the emaciated hooker fidgeted nervously.

Stanley plowed on. "Did you know, Detective, that my client is indeed a hair dresser?"

"No, sir, I did not know that, Mr. Nyland."

"And, in fact, you misunderstood her when she offered you a blow *dry* for fifteen dollars?"

"No, Mr. Nyland, she plainly offered me a blow *job*. Besides, sir, what hair dressers solicit on the street corner?"

The attorney had done his job, in attempting to give his client the best possible defense. He had tried to muddy the waters of justice.

The judge was still grinning as he found her guilty

and ordered her to pay a fine.

COP-IN-A-BOX.

"How can I arrest hookers for solicitation when all of them on Ponce know me?" I lamented that October day in 1983.

I was even more tired of undercover work after thirteen months. Homicide was where I wanted to be, but the brass kept me languishing busting whores.

We were off-duty at the bar at Manuel's, and Bill McCloskey, the head bartender, was listening to me bitch. "If all the whores know you're a cop," he offered, idly wiping the sheeny bar, "maybe I can get solicited and you can bust 'em."

Like in the cartoons, a light bulb popped above my head. "If you want to do it," I said, "there *is* a way."

Saturday afternoon, when my tour of duty began, I met Mack. "First we have to find a big cardboard box," I said.

"What will you do with a cardboard box?"

"I'll cut a peep hole in it. We'll put it in the back of your pickup truck with me inside. You pick up a hooker and I can hear when she propositions you. Then I'll jump out and arrest her!"

The bearded bartender grinned.

"Just don't pick up a he-she," I warned. "They like to fight."

Sears had a huge, brick complex on Ponce de Leon Avenue that, a decade later, the city would purchase and convert into City Hall East. The building would also come to crunch the bones of one good cop. From this address I commandeered an empty refrigerator box. Cutting a peep hole, I positioned myself in the bed of Mack's truck and told him to have at it.

He drove around a long time, me sitting cross-legged on the hard metal floor. Through the open vent in his back window, Mack finally told me a hooker was flagging him down.

I felt the truck stop. "Want a date?" a voice asked and I tried to see who it was.

"Sure," Mack said.

"You're not a cop, are you?"

"Hell, no. I'm a bartender."

The door opened and I saw a hooker I didn't recognize slide into the seat. She had long blonde hair, short dress, and alluring cleavage.

The hooker directed the bartender to an alley behind some flea-bag apartments, and he turned off the engine.

I had already warned Bill against entrapment, that the prostitute must be the one to bring up sex for money.

"What are you looking for, honey?" she asked.

Pause. "Uh. The regular," he stammered.

"The regular *what?*"

"You *know.* What you do for all the guys."

"You sure you ain't a cop?"

"I told you. I'm a bartender. I'm just shy."

This seemed to go on and on, and my legs were very uncomfortable.

"You look like a big ole lumberjack."

"I've been told that before. I'm from Minnesota."

"Oh, in that case, how about I give you a blowjob for twenty-five bucks?"

Bingo! I had heard enough to arrest her for solicitation of prostitution. Throwing the box up, I exclaimed: "Police officer! You're under arrest!"

In shock, the hooker looked at me and my gold badge through the rear window. Then she was out the door and running. Leaping to my feet to give chase, I found my legs had gone to sleep from sitting cross-legged so long.

The only thing left of the hooker was a pair of garish silver slippers.

****

My unhappiness working UC finally ended. Major "Short Billy" Neikirk (*not* Officer Billy "Too Tall" King from Zone 2) called me into his office on the third floor of headquarters. He was in charge of the Crimes Against Persons section.

"I understand you'd like a shot at Homicide," he said in his gravely voice, lighting a long cigarette.

Scooting forward in my seat, I said: "Yes, *sir.*"

"I've got some good reports about your work, except that you don't seem to like UC work. I'm an old Homicide man myself."

I already knew about his rapport with the Homicide guys. When I was in the Homicide office giving my statement about shooting the armed robber, I watched as two laughing detectives hauled

Neikirk□s desk and chair from his office. A third detective showed me a doll's desk and chair just before he laid them down on the major's floor.

"We zing Short Billy all the time about his height," he said, running to look out the window, making sure Neikirk was still out of sight. "Last month we picked up his laundry and switched his slacks for some khaki shorts!"

"I can tell by your smile," Neikirk said to me, "that this transfer out of UC agrees with you."

"You're very observant, sir," I said, stifling my grin, returning to the present.

"I want you to work temporarily in Robbery first." He stubbed the cigarette out in his ashtray. "Then you can go to Homicide."

Goodbye to blue jeans and tee-shirts and hello to a suit and tie.

Throwing my junk into a cardboard box I'd gotten from Manuel's, I moved down the hall at police headquarters to my new office.

ANOTHER PAROLE BOARD SUCCESS.

Once he realized he had walked into my trap, it was too late. Fearful as I watched his prison-muscles flex against the seemingly tiny handcuffs, I realized that Allen Adams was a raping, killing machine of frightening proportions.

The twenty-one-year-old was six-foot-two, two-hundred-and-thirty pounds and his hair had not yet grown from his last session with the prison barber.

"You know," Fugitive Detective Stapp said to me. "I've seen his face before." Stapp searched through his briefcase until he withdrew a wanted flyer. "I bet this is gonna be him."

The flyer was from Sex Crimes. It bore a drawing of a suspect who had brutally raped a

Georgia Tech coed after shooting her boyfriend in the leg and making him watch the rape of his girlfriend.

But my warrant for the goliath was for armed robbery, agg assault, kidnapping, and auto theft.

On November 29, 1984, around 9:15 P.M., sixty-year-old John Hale pulled his '76 Ford Granada into the parking lot of the Baptist Towers retirement home where he lived with his wife, Hilda.

Parking in his assigned space, the white-haired man climbed from his car and opened the back seat door to pull out his groceries. A black male holding a pistol startled Mr. Hale when he came up from behind him. As the victim looked around for help, a muscular black male, a revolver in his right hand, joined his partner.

"Please don't hurt me," the old man begged as they pushed him into the back seat of his own car and slammed the door against him.

The kidnappers drove him down the street, then onto 166 eastbound, then to I75 north. They exited on Northside Drive, in the northwest part of

Atlanta, and the southside resident then lost track of where they were taking him.

"Come up off your wallet, old man."

"Take anything you want," the frightened man pleaded, handing over his wallet with palsied hand. "Just please don't kill me."

The muscular one said to him: "If you tell anything to the poelease we'll come back an' *kill* you. We know where you live."

The Granada abruptly stopped and they pushed out Mr. Hale. Lost and terrified, he looked for lights, people, anyone who could help him. He stepped off the road into some grass and slipped down a hill just as a shot rang out from his fleeing car. If he had not stumbled just then, he would have been shot in the back of the head.

****

The Robbery sarge assigned me to the case. When I interviewed the short old man, he told me the first perp was thin and a little nervous. "But the heavily muscled one, he seemed quite confident. I'd say he's done this sort of crime before but the smaller one was new at it."

Mr. Hale gave me a list of items stored in his trunk: a set of Tourney golf clubs in a tan bag, a new golf rain suit, a golf trophy from the Senior Golfers Association of Atlanta, a gavel inscribed "John S. Hale," a wooden cane with a round brass head, and a small tool box.

If I was to get a break in this case, it would probably be from catching the perps in the stolen Granada. I had all six patrol zones alerted to the lookout, and then I entered its tag and VIN onto the NCIC computer system.

Sunday, three days later, Radio notified me that a Zone 4 beat cop had recovered the stolen car the night before. He had found it wrapped around a telephone pole on Martin Luther King Jr. Drive, only a few miles from where the victim had been let out. No one was with the car.

It had already been impounded, so I went to the impound lot.

Ducking my head into the mangled wreck, I noted blood splattered profusely on the front seat and front floorboard. The steering wheel was damaged. The front windshield was shattered.

Radioing for an ID tech, I requested photos of the car. "And, Shirley, I also need you to take blood samples from the interior."

****

Grady Memorial Hospital, a huge edifice in Downtown, was the free clinic. I drove to the emergency room around 5:00 P.M. Seeing a nurse I knew from Manuel's, I went to her. She was busy with about thirty injured patients. "Terri, I need to look through the blue sheets starting last night."

"Wait for me in the break room," she said, pushing limp hair from her face. "I'll bring them to you."

Sitting in the room, where two nurses smoked and discussed a planned vacation to Cancun, I lit a cigarette myself. When Terri laid a stack of blue forms in front of me, she said, "Yell if you need me," and returned to the chaos of the ER.

I searched every form for a black male complaining of the type injuries the wrecked Granada would have caused. Thirty minutes later I discovered a likely suspect. One Allen Adams had come to the ER with facial lacerations and a large contusion on his chest. Setting his form aside, I continued to search. Reviewing the last blue sheet, I only had the one set aside. Allen Adams.

Returning the stack to Terri, I showed her Adams' sheet. "Can you decipher who the treating physician was?"

"Sure. Doctor Montgomery. Says so right here."

"Is he still on-duty?"

"Sure is. I just saw him with a tibia down the hall."

After Dr. Montgomery, a pale, thin man with a

raspy voice and curly brown beard, was finished ministering the broken tibia, I approached him. "Doc, I know you're busy as hell but I need some help in a nasty robbery case."

Checking his watch as if to tell me he was on an extremely tight schedule, he said: "Make it brief."

Showing him the blue sheet, he immediately remembered the patient who had come in that morning. "He was a really *big* guy," he said, nodding.

"How did he say he got his injuries?"

"He told me six dudes jumped on him. Big as he is, I guess he thought we wouldn't believe just one or *two* could whip him."

"So you didn't believe his story?"

"I did not, no. But it isn't my job to believe or disbelieve patients. Just treat them."

"Do you think his injuries were more consistent with a car wreck?"

"It *is* possible, but no doctor could make a definite ruling on something like that. Now that you mention it, I do remember thinking his facial lacerations appeared to be glass cuts."

"Like from hitting a car windshield?"

"Right," he said, nodding his head.

"And the large contusion on Adam's chest could likely have been caused by impact from the steering wheel of a car?"

"That would be logical. But it would still be speculation."

****

Going to our ID section, I found that Adams should still be in prison serving a term for murder. Only four years ago he had been plea-bargained down from murder to voluntary manslaughter and received a ten-year sentence. He had been paroled last month, after serving four years.

His parole officer described the killing as drug-related. "He had been selling crack with the victim, who apparently ripped him off for some money. Adams got a shotgun and went after him, kicking in the front door of his mama's apartment. He found the other kid cowering in a closet. He begged Adams not to kill him, but Adams blew him away with the shotgun."

"Well, he is a certain candidate for early parole," I said sarcastically.

Taking Adams' mugshot, I put together a photo lineup for Mr. Hale to review. His wife Hilda welcomed me into their apartment in Baptist Towers. It looked like anybody's grandparents' home with framed portraits of their grown children, and lots of photos of the grandkids. Fragile porcelain knickknacks seemed to watch us from everywhere. Their home smelled of cinnamon.

Hilda sitting next to him on the sofa, my victim stopped when he turned to Adams' photo.

"That's him," he declared. "He was one of them. He was the big, confident one."

I immediately secured an arrest warrant for Allen Adams.

Calling his parole officer again, I told her I had

a warrant for Adams' arrest. "Why don't you call him and have him come to your office," I suggested. "Tell him it's just a routine interview."

"As big and violent as Adams is, you don't want to try and take him down on the street. I don't blame you. Adams scares the hell out of *me.*"

When Adams entered the parole office, two Fugitive detectives fell quickly on him and cuffed his huge arms before he knew what was happening. He looked at us with eyeballs that seemed as small as almonds in his big head.

Mirandizing Adams, he said he wasn't going to make a statement about any robbery. Then he asked: "What kinda evidence you got against me?"

"I've got the wrecked Granada, and the driver of that car obviously got injured. I know that *you* went to the Grady ER with lacerations and contusions on the same day as that wreck."

Looking confident, he asked: "When did I come into Grady?"

"At 1:45 P.M.."

"What time did the wreck happen?"

"At 7:45 A.M.."

He immediately rejoined: "Oh, I was supposed to have sat at home all day and bled until I went to Grady?"

That statement suggested to me that Adams knew the wreck occurred about five hours prior to his father bringing him into the Grady ER. His pointed questions were obviously intended to show me he had what he considered an alibi.

****

My victim, Mr. Hale, wasn't the only person to identify Adams when we conducted a physical lineup at the city jail. The Georgia Tech coed, who was raped while her wounded boyfriend was forced to watch, also identified Adams as her assailant.

The state crime lab concluded that the blood I recovered from the wrecked Granada must have come from Allen Adams.

For the armed robbery, he was sentenced to life in prison. For the agg assault he was given a concurrent life sentence. For the kidnapping, rape, and aggravated sodomy of the coed, Adams was given three more life sentences -- again to run concurrent with the other life sentences. For the kidnaping, armed robbery, and agg assault on the coed's boyfriend, he was given three more concurrent life sentences. For the charges of possession of a firearm by a convicted felon, Adams was sentenced to ten years to run concurrent with all the other charges. Had the sentences instead been consecutive, he would not be eligible so soon for another early parole. In prison, his parole officer told me, he went back to lifting weights and playing football with his fellow inmates. If he gets out early again, he'll have the build of the Terminator.

PIEDMONT JOE.

"We've got a problem," the ADA called me at the office to say. "I can't locate the gunshot victim in the Stop N Go robbery. His testimony is *crucial*. Without him, the defendant walks."

"This shooter *can't* walk," I protested.

"It's out of my hands without the victim's testimony."

"I'll find him." Until then, I thought the September 27, 1985, case was sewn-up. I was wrong.

When shots rang out at the Stop N Go, three teenagers who were playing video games fled into the back freezer. A cabbie pulled into the parking lot in time to hear the shots through the glass front, and radioed his dispatcher.

The words crackling over my car radio got my adrenaline cranking: "All detective units, a signal thirty-six with shots fired at Stop N Go, six-sixty-four

North Highland Northeast." A robbery-in-progress call is one we cops fly to.

When I slid my unmarked unit into the small lot, however, it was obvious the perp had gotten away. Two beat cars were already there, parked at defensive angles in case they encountered the armed robber.

Hurrying over to the uniform officers, I saw a portly man with short dark hair lying on the cement stoop outside the store. Arthur Kaplan, a part-time municipal court judge who volunteered his emergency medical services as a Rescue unit, was rapidly pressing bundles of gauze to bleeding wounds in the man's stomach and chest. Arthur's white hair looked like tufts of cotton balls.

"This is the cashier," one of the cops told me. "He was shot by the robber."

"Are there any witnesses?"

Pointing to three white teenagers, two boys and a girl, the officer said: "They were inside. I haven't interviewed them yet."

Kaplan, wearing his trademark blood-soaked, white smock, shouted over his shoulder: "Get me an ETA on the four!" But the ambulance pulled up screaming at that very moment.

Approaching the shivering kids, I asked: "Did you guys see what happened?"

Cameron, a fourteen-year-old high school student, spoke up immediately. "I was watching Donald and Jennifer playing the video games and then two black guys came in, they walked in front of me, the first black guy got some ice cream and then the second black man came in and got some ice cream, too. One reason that made me notice them was that he bumped into me as he was passing by. Later on, we heard something that sounded like fire crackers, I walked up toward the front a little bit, and the black man was yelling at the cashier to open up the register. Then I heard Jennifer and Donald running toward the back, and I noticed that the guy had a gun, I ran back to the back, and I saw a freezer. I got inside the freezer. After that I heard several other shots from a gun, I looked out the door, and I saw the black guy jumping up and down, yelling at the cashier. Then I went back into the freezer, and about two minutes later I stepped out with Jennifer and Donald. We walked up to the front and we saw the man behind the counter bleeding. The guy that bumped into me was the same one that I saw with the gun, shooting the cashier."

A mild breeze blew through, making some newsprint do cartwheels through the lot on the corner of North Highland and Blueridge Avenue.

"You three live around here?"

"I do," Cameron said. "On Saint Charles."

"I just live a block away," Donald said, pointing north with a trembling, thin arm. "But this is my girlfriend. She lives in Cobb County."

This area, about three miles from the Strip, was close to my beat when I was a patrolman. Called Poncey-Highlands, it was a mixture of lower middle-class homes, a lot of Georgia State University students in apartments, and kids in droves on skateboards, like these three witnesses. But there were also several halfway houses in the vicinity, and a lot of lowlife street people from Ponce de Leon Avenue, only one block north. Manuel's, our favorite watering hole, was two blocks south.

"Cartwright, can I talk to you?" someone called, and I saw Kenny, a black, diminutive, thirty-three-year-old cabbie who was a regular on these streets.

Going over to him, I shook his hand. "Did you see what went down, Kenny?"

"Hell, Cartwright, *I'm* the one called it in."

"Yeah?"

"See, I was just pulling into the parking lot when I heard this *bang, bang-bang* from inside. I had my window down because uh how hot it is this afternoon. I could see inside the store and a black male was stooped behind the counter, screaming at the attendant. Something to the effect of `Open it now, open it now.'

"I radioed to my dispatcher and told him there was a robbery in progress and that shots was fired. I backed out of the parking lot and the black male started out the door and he began stuffing the money and the gun under his shirt. He just strolled out, Cartwright, like he was real calm. He made a right turn around the building, and I circled around the left of the building and the dude was *gone*. He disappeared."

Knowing that Kenny knew the local players, the hookers, the pimps, the junkies, I asked if he recognized the shooter.

Shrugging, he said, "I seen the guy in the neighborhood before."

"You know his name?"

"I don't think so, but he do be around."

"Thanks, Kenny. I'm going to need you and those three kids to make a statement at the Robbery office. I'll get an officer to take ya'll down."

"No need, Cartwright. I know the way. I'll drive my cab."

When I returned to the victim, he was already on a gurney about to be lifted into the Grady

Memorial Hospital ambulance. An EMT shoved an oxygen mask over the man's face, so I knew I wouldn't get anything from him now.

"Did any of you guys get an ID on him?"

"I got his wallet," one of the cops said, reading, with difficulty, the victim's name. "Mohammed Malick. Apparently he's a native of Pakistan."

As the ambulance went screaming away with the victim inside, Kaplan stood beside me, stripping off his bloodied plastic gloves. "He's low, Cartwright. I don't know if he's going to make it. It looks like he's got two bullets in his belly and one in his chest. Any leads on the perp?"

"Seems like he's a local, Arthur. This being close to my old beat, I should get a name on him soon."

Mallory, an ID tech, pulled up to work the crime scene.

Before pushing through the bloodied glass door, I told the uniforms: "Nobody comes in here."

****

The checkout counter was to the left as we entered the door. A pushup frozen dessert stood erect next to the cash register. Below that, a magazine display was speckled with blood. The *National Enquirer* heralded: ROCK HUDSON -- THE FINAL DAYS. Another tabloid proclaimed: TWO-HEADED BABY ALIVE AND KICKING. *Reader's Digest* promised: BE FIT FOR LIFE!

Seeing a security camera on the wall pointing down made me hope we had our shooter on film.

Working the crime scene, I discovered what appeared to be a bullet hole n the wall behind where the cashier, who was working alone that day, had been standing. Mallory photographed the hole and we took measurements of how far away it was from the counter.

The cash register drawer was open and the register keys were broken and strewn all over the floor. Mallory photographed these and the frozen pushup sitting mysteriously on the counter. If the cashier lived, I hoped he would explain the significance of these items.

The blood on the door was where the cashier pushed through it after being shot.

Mallory dusted the door and the entire counter and register for latents but none of value were found. The identity of the shooter would not come from fingerprints.

A zone cop stuck his head through the door. "Cartwright. A company representative is here. She wants to know what happened."

"Send her in."

A crowd of curiosity-seekers watched from behind yellow crime scene tape as the rep, a middle-aged lady in a maroon dress, was escorted through the door. She was visibly shaken at the sight of blood. After explaining to her all I knew, I asked: "That surveillance camera. I need to get the film out."

"Oh, that thing," she said, embarrassed. "We

haven't had film in there for months."

"Great," I muttered. "Look. We're almost through here, so I'm turning custody of the store over to you."

****

Swinging by Grady Hospital, I found Mr. Malick was in Emergency Surgery in critical condition. Before leaving, I took possession of the three bullets removed from him. If a gun was ever recovered, we might be able to match the slugs to it.

After completing the preliminary paperwork, and reviewing the written statements from the four witnesses, I could at last hit the streets looking for leads.

The next day, Saturday, I corralled Brenda, the hooker who☐d been raped by Ned Lansing. Hookers are always good snitches because they don't want a cop hanging around. It's bad for business.

"I seen Piedmont Joe last night with a pistol

and some money," Brenda said, leaning in my open car window. Her breath was like a stench, and I could imagine it was from any of the dozen blow jobs she'd given that day. "Joe was talkin' something about the Stop N Go."

I knew Piedmont Joe well. His real name was Jason Anthony Kirkland, AKA Joseph Edward Moody and Joseph Copeland. "Piedmont" was the name of an Atlanta street where Joe hung-out in his earlier years.

He was a known pimp with a bad record. I had sent him to prison only three years previously, for armed robbery and agg assault. For that offense he had been sentenced to five years in prison -- so he was out on early parole for that when the Stop N Go crime went down. His rap sheet also included thefts, aggravated assaults, drug offenses, and pandering. Only thirty-one, he had been busy all his life.

Making a photo lineup of mug shots of five different black males, including Piedmont Joe, I hurried to Grady Hospital. In the ICU, the victim was, remarkably, still alive.

"Mr. Malick," I said. "I'm the detective working this case. Do you feel up to looking at some photographs?"

"Yes, I will do," the forty-seven-year-old Pakistani man said, though he seemed weak.

Handing him the photos, he studied number one, then studied number two. When he turned to number three, he exclaimed immediately: "This is the one! This is the one who shot me!"

It was the mug shot of Piedmont Joe.

****

From his hospital bed, Mr. Malick was able to tell me what happened.

"I had just been dealing with a customer when a black American came to the counter with a bar of ice cream." I realized that was the pushup we had discovered and photographed. "He left the ice cream bar on the counter and came to the other end of the counter and opened fire on me after demanding the money from me.

"When I was wounded badly, he came forward and broke the cash register and took the money and ran away. The customers who had hidden themselves in the cold room came out. I myself came out from the store and shouted for help. Somebody called the police."

"How did he break the cash register?" I asked.

"He hit it with his gun," he said, pantomiming it from his hospital bed.

That explained the register keys strewn behind the bloodied counter.

Going into more detail, Malick said Joe put the ice cream on the counter and pulled out a handgun, demanding the money. Nervous, Malick fumbled with the keys. Joe responded by firing one round which missed the cashier but shrapneled, a fragment hitting the cashier painfully in the back of the head.

This is what the three kids playing video thought was a firecracker. When they looked toward the counter, however, and saw Joe firing three rounds into his victim, the kids fled into the back cooler.

Malick, now shot twice in the abdomen and once in the chest, watched dazed as Joe banged on the register with the butt of his gun, trying to force it open. The drawer finally sprang open and Joe snatched $205 and fled out the door.

"There was a cabbie in the parking lot," I told Mr. Malick. "He had his dispatcher call us for you."

"God bless him."

Before I left, Malick said: "You know, I must have a major surgery done to me. The Almighty God has blessed me with new life."

****

From Grady, I went straight to where Cameron lived with his parents. Showing the photo lineup to the high school student, he immediately tapped his forefinger onto Piedmont Joe's face.

****

I sat rubbing the ears of the huge, white Labrador retriever as its master, Judge Andy Mickle, signed my arrest warrant for Piedmont Joe. This being Saturday, I had to find a judge at home.

Joe wasn't hard to find. We snatched him up as he emerged from a suspected shooting gallery, where addicts go to inject their drugs.

"Assume the position, Joe," I told him, and he put his hands on the wall as I searched him. Mirandizing him, I then asked: "Where's the gun, Joe?"

"What gun, Cartwright?" he asked, his dark eyes looking malicious.

"The gun you shot the cashier with yesterday."

He didn't seem surprised. "I ain't did that, Cartwright, but I know who did."

Placing the handcuffs on him, I said: "So, tell me, Joe."

"Cartwright, you know the dude that did it. His name's Willie. He hangs out at the corner. He drives that blue car with the broken window."

Piedmont Joe was booked for armed robbery and aggravated assault. Later that evening, I repeated Joe's story about "Willie" to another informant on Ponce de Leon.

"Naw, Cartwright," the CI said with a chortle. "Willie beat the shit outta Joe the day before the Stop N Go, an' stole Joe's old lady from him. Since then folk on the street be callin' him `Chump' Joe instead uh `Piedmount.'"

"So Joe probably felt he had to do something to bolster his image on the street," I surmised.

"You got dat right."

And that's what led to Mr. Malick being shot.

With this new information, I talked to Joe in the city jail.

"Naw, naw, Cartwright, man, you *know* what kinda robberies I do. I use muscle. Have you ever known me to use a gun?"

"What about a month ago, Joe? When some Vice detectives busted you on the street at four in the morning. You were carrying a two-by-four."

"Wuddn't no *gun.*"

"The last time *I* arrested you, Joe, you robbed your old lady's trick and cut him with a knife when he resisted. Then you shoved him through a plate glass window."

"Wuddn't no *gun.*"

Another snitch told me Joe had stolen two handguns on the very day of the Stop N Go robbery. "Joe was tryin' to sell them guns," he said. "They was a .38 and a .32."

The handgun used to shoot Mr. Malick was never found.

****

Municipal court, in those days, was held in three cramped rooms on the second floor of police headquarters Downtown. There were never enough fans or room deodorizers to counteract the cloying smell of body odor.

Prisoners were locked in a bulletproof cage on the opposite side of the court room from the pews where the cops and lawyers sat.

When guards brought in the prisoners, I watched my victim's face to see if he recognized Joe. Malick became suddenly agitated, pointing vehemently toward the cage, and saying something to friends sitting in the audience with him.

Going over to him, I asked: "Do you see the man who shot you, Mister Malick?"

"Yes, yes, oh *yes.* The fourth from the left in the last row." He was, of course, pointing out Piedmont Joe.

During the preliminary hearing, when he was asked if he was sure that the defendant was the one who shot him, Mr. Malick emphatically answered: "When I go to sleep at night I keep seeing his face. Whenever I close my eyes I see him. *He* is the one who shot me," he declared, pointing to Joe.

As Piedmont Joe, and all his other aliases, were bound-over to the Fulton County Grand Jury for indictment, I felt confident he would finally be put away for a long time.

Then the ADA called me, telling me that Mr. Malick's home number was disconnected.

Alarmed, I called the corporate offices of Stop N Go. "He's moved back to Pakistan," I was told.

"Just to *visit,* right? He is coming back, right?"

"It doesn't sound like it. He's moved back with his family. They live out in the jungle, or whatever it is they have over there in Pakistan. I have a telephone number. It's at a store in the village."

Calling the number in Pakistan, I luckily found someone who could speak a little English. They said they would send a boy to the Malick house and fetch him back. When I called again in fifteen minutes, Malick was summoned to the phone.

"I had to come back to bury my mother. I will have to have my major surgeries done here."

"But we *need* you for superior court."

"American justice is good. You will have done the right thing."

"But, Mister Malick, the way our justice system works, you are the one who must testify about what he did to you."

"American justice is good. You will have done the right thing."

I couldn't get him to understand. He definitely was never returning to the United States.

"I'll have to talk to the assistant district attorney who's trying the case. Can you at least send me a written statement about the robbery and the shooting?"

I immediately called the ADA. He was not pleased. "If the defendant wants a jury trial, I'll have to drop the charges."

"I can't believe this."

"Due to the seriousness of the crime, I recommended a lengthy prison term. He *wants* a trial."

"And there's no way we can wing it with a

written statement and my testimony?"

"We *must* have the victim's testimony for a trial."

"Maybe we can fool Joe. See if he'll cop a plea?"

"He wants a trial."

"Do you think his attorney found out Malick's left the country?"

"Sure the hell sounds like it."

And so it went, much to my horror. The charges against Piedmont Joe were dropped and he returned like a shot to the streets. I still saw him quite often. He'd been arrested for drunk and disorderly charges, and my snitches told me he has been rolling drunks for their money. By doing that, he ensured that his victims were not able to identify him in court.

Leaving the court house, I was stomping its marble floor.

****

My anger was somewhat abated by the news of my next transfer. I was finally getting into what I thought was the big time -- the Homicide squad.

JUDICIAL GIBBERISH.

Walking into the superior court room, I saw the judge was taking a plea. The ADA I needed to speak to about a pending murder case was at the podium, facing a contrite-looking defendant and his defense attorney.

The ADA intoned: "The negotiated plea with this defendant, your honor, is that his probation be revoked, and then suspended."

It took me a second to figure out what that meant. The guy was already on probation when arrested for his current felony charge. By state law that means his probation must be revoked and he serves the balance of time in his previous sentence. The plea did that. Then the ADA suspended the revocation.

It almost made me dizzy contemplating the meaning. As a Zen master might say: Can you envision the picture of a door revolving?

A WOMAN OF COLD STEEL.

Seeing the old lady's battered face as the EMTs carried her out of her bedroom, I knew I would be looking for a monster.

By the end of the night, encountering the victim's gray-and-red-haired daughter, I *knew* I'd found the monster.

****

Ruth Rose, a live-in nurse, attended church services every Sunday morning and evening, and Tuesday and Thursday evening. That's the few times the slight, vibrant, fifty-year-old black woman left her patient alone in her house in the upper-middle-class Morningside neighborhood, just north of Midtown. Mrs. Grace Carter [names have been changed in this chapter] was a bedridden invalid and every time she fell out of bed Ruth had to call the Atlanta Fire Department to lift her back between the covers.

As Ruth parked her car at Mrs. Carter's, where Ruth also lived, her eye noticed the digital clock before the numbers 9:09 flicked to 9:10.

Walking up the stone walk in the back, she noticed all the house lights were on as she had left them two hours ago to attend Tuesday church service.

With shock, Ruth saw the back door standing open.

Rushing into the house and through the kitchen to Mrs. Carter's dark bedroom, Ruth quickly clicked on the ceiling light. She saw her patient in her bed. Then she saw the bloodied pillow next to her head.

Before dialing 911, Ruth checked to make sure

the eighty-year-old lady was breathing.

****

I hadn't jogged since graduating the Academy eight years before, and my 6'3" frame was a good thirty pounds overweight. A buddy who worked Zone 2, Sergeant Ronnie Shaw, known as Whale since his teens, suggested we jog three nights a week after our shift ended at midnight.

Whale, despite his bulk, was a natural runner. There was a mile-long service road snaking around one of the city's reservoirs on the northside. It was situated on a hilltop so that, as we jogged, we could see the lights of the Downtown cityscape shimmering in the nocturnal lake. Over our huffing, we could hear crickets and frogs calling.

I also attacked my shaking belly with a diet of vegetables. When it was my choice where Ronnie and I ate on duty, we usually met and he'd drive us to Piccadilly's. When it was Ronnie's turn to choose we almost always ended up at Zesto's. That's where we were heading in his patrol car that evening on April 22, 1986. We were about a mile away when the call came over Ronnie's radio: "A signal forty-four with a four dispatched," which meant a robbery with injuries and an ambulance was responding.

Arriving almost simultaneously with us was Officer Billy "Too Tall" King. I saw Ruth standing in the front door of the house on the hill. She was gesturing for us to hurry.

"It's Miz Carter!" she exclaimed. "Some robbers beat her bad!"

Rushing into the room just as a tiny Manchester dog began barking madly at us from the kitchen, I first saw the pudgy lady lying face-up in bed. Her face had been badly beaten and was covered with blood. The left side of her face was so badly swollen that she could not open that eye. A puddle of blood formed a halo behind her head on the pillow. She was moaning through bloodied lips. I noticed red marks on both sides of her pale neck.

"There's an ambulance on the way for you, ma'am," I assured her. "Can you tell us what happened?"

She seemed dazed. "Was laying in bed with the lights out. Somebody threw a pillow over my head. Jumped on top me. Tried to smother me. Then beat me in my face really *hard*. Then tried to strangle me." The bloodied pillow next to her seemed to come from a second single bed which was pushed next to the one she lay in.

The dog continued to bark angrily at us.

"Can you describe who attacked you?"

"No. The hall light was the only light on, and I had my eyes closed."

"I found the back door open," Ruth volunteered. "When I left, it was locked. And look here." The live-in caretaker pointed to the floor at the foot of the bed. "It's Miz Carter's pocket book layin' on the floor."

"Your dog," I said, "does it stay in the house?"

"Yes," Ruth answered for the victim who was

writing in pain. Over the barks of the small but loud dog, I heard the rescue wagon's approaching siren.

"Mrs. Carter," I said, drawing close so she could hear me. "Did you hear your dog bark when you were being attacked?"

"No."

"You didn't hear the dog bark at your intruders?"

"She never barked once."

I stood up straight. "Does the dog usually bark at strangers?"

"Always," answered Ruth.

Two fire department EMTs entered and we cops walked into the kitchen to get out of their way.

Having a love for dogs, I offered my hand to the yapping pooch. Suspicious at first, she finally stopped barking and allowed me to rub her head. Picking the Manchester up and scratching behind its black ear, I walked to the kitchen door. "Whale," I said to Sergeant Shaw, "I don't see any sign of forced entry to this door."

Shining his flashlight over every inch of the screen and wooden door, we concluded there was no sign of forced entry.

Still cradling the family dog, Whale and I examined every exterior window and door. No sign of forced entry was to be found. "Something's not right here," I said, and Whale agreed.

Back inside the house, Ruth had examined Mrs. Carter's purse. "There was three dollar bills in it when I left," she said. "Now they be gone. And somebody opened some draws in my room."

Her room was next to her patient's. Two drawers were pulled out. Peering into them, I saw everything within was orderly. No sign of rummaging.

Looking through every room, I found the house was in immaculate shape. There were radios, TV sets, and silverware. None had been moved.

"Mother?" I heard a woman's voice call.

"That's Deidra," Ruth told me. "Miz Carter's daughter. I called her right after I called the poelease."

Deidra entered the bedroom where the EMTs were gently placing her mother onto a gurney. Deidra looked calm and reposed.

At last putting down the victim's dog, it saw Deidra, then fled to a faraway room as if hiding.

"What happened to my mother?"

"I'm Detective Cartwright. I work the Aggravated Assaults / Homicide squad," I said, studying the fiftyish woman with short gray-and-red hair brushed away from her face. She held her head erect in a haughty manner. "Someone assaulted your mother. Tried to smother her, then beat her in the face with an unknown object, then tried to strangle her."

Still not going to her mother's side, the daughter said: "You think it might be related to those elderly women being strangled in the housing projects? I saw that on the news." Her words were slurred and I could smell alcohol.

"I don't think so," I said. "But it's too early to tell."

As the EMTs were taking Mrs. Carter to the ambulance, Deidra declared that she would survey the house to determine what the burglars may have stolen.

With Deidra out of the room, Ruth came close to me and whispered: "Deidra's got a drinking problem."

"Do you think *she* may have done this to her mother, Ruth?"

She gave me a look that seemed to say: Of *course* she could.

****

An ID tech arrived to dust for latent fingerprints.

"Nothing," he finally declared, stripping the plastic gloves from his hands.

Canvassing the neighborhood, the next-door neighbors reported seeing no suspicious people or hearing anything out of the ordinary. This was a quiet neighborhood of retired people, lawyers, and business people with young families.

The family directly behind the widow Carter's home was having a birthday party for one of their three-year-old daughters.

"Would you like some cake, Detective?" the lady of the house asked merrily.

"No, thank you." She was shocked to hear of the attack on her neighbor.

"Was Ruth there?"

"Ruth was away at church. Did anyone here see or hear anything suspicious?"

Surveying her house full of happy partiers, she said: "We've had guests arriving and departing for *hours.* We haven't noticed anything untoward."

Whale drove me back to the Zone 2 precinct where I'd left my detective car.

****

At the Piedmont Hospital Emergency Room, I awaited the attending physician. When he came from triage, I asked what he could tell me about the wounds.

"I noted abrasions on the patient's left cheek and nose, which are similar to rug burns."

"Could that have been caused by a pillowcase?"

Scratching his stiff black beard, he nodded. "It could. I've seen it in elderly patients who fall from their bed and get a bad burn across the rug."

"But Mrs. Carter's an invalid, she couldn't have fallen from bed and gotten back in alone," I said.

"Plus I noted severe swelling of the left eye and cheek as if she had been struck with something like a rock. And there's definite indication of attempted strangulation on both sides of the patient's neck. The blood vessels of her eyes also show hemorrhaging that is indicative of a strangulation attempt. Whoever did all that to that little old lady is a *monster.* I hope you get them."

When I saw Deidra stumbling down the bright hospital corridor, she was my main suspect. But I needed a confession. Asking her in a comforting voice to join me in a private office, I tried to finesse her.

"Would you like some coffee?"

She shook her head as she sat in a chair and I perched on the edge of a desk.

"I'm a civil attorney, you know," she said.

"I didn't know," I said. "We've gathered some evidence at the crime scene," I lied. "Once I send that to the state crime lab, maybe they'll come up with a suspect."

"I have a friend at the state crime lab," she volunteered, holding her head back in that haughty manner of hers. "Doctor Howard. Know him?"

"Never heard of him."

"He's told me some things about crime scene evidence."

Steering the conversation back to her mother, I tried a ploy I hoped would trigger her confession. "Whoever did this horrible thing to your mother, Deidra, will surely burn in hell."

She broke into tears. *Here,* I thought, *comes*

the confession. But the tears stopped as quickly as they had started. "My mother's going to die -- I don't mean tonight -- but she's very old and sick."

Deidra, I realized then, was a woman made of cold steel.

****

The next afternoon I visited Mrs. Carter in her private hospital room. Standing over her bed, holding the old lady's hand, was a pretty red-haired woman about thirty years old who turned quickly to see who entered the room.

"I'm Detective Cartwright," I told her. "I'm investigating Mrs. Carter's assault."

She smiled. "I'm Karen Zenda, her granddaughter."

"Then you're -- Deidra's daughter?"

"Yes," she said and lowered her head as if embarrassed.

Crossing to the opposite side of the bed, I saw

the entire left side of the victim's face was bandaged. She was staring at the ceiling with her one good eye. Occasionally she would turn her eye briefly on me as I spoke, then returned her stare to the ceiling.

"How are you feeling today, Mrs. Carter?"

"Bad."

"I'm sorry to hear that. You'll be out of here really soon," I said, although she would end up there for two weeks. "I know this is painful, ma'am, but can you remember any more at all about what happened last night? Did you ever see as much as a hand of your attacker?"

"No."

"You remember I asked you last night if your little dog ever barked at your attacker?"

"She didn't bark."

"Mrs. Carter -- how do you and your daughter Deidra get along?"

Karen shivered. Looking at her face, I could tell she wanted to relate something to me. "Detective," she finally said. "Can I speak to you in the hall?"

"Certainly."

"I'll be right back, Meemaw. I'll just be outside your door if you need me."

In the hospital corridor, with strolling nurses and orderlies pushing trays of supplies and food, Deidra's daughter bluntly asked: "Do you think my mother attacked my Meemaw?"

Hesitating, I decided to be honest. "I think there's a good possibility. There's circumstantial evidence, but not enough to bring a charge. What do *you* think?"

Karen crossed her arms below her breasts, as though giving herself a hug. "My mother's an alcoholic. She was an attorney but was disbarred because of her erratic behavior."

"She told me last night she was an attorney. She didn't tell me she'd been disbarred."

"Well, she has. She's been working in a real estate office but was just fired."

"Do you live with her?"

With a bitter smile, she answered: "Uh-uh. No

way. As soon as I was legal, I moved out of that hell house. So did my brother."

"You didn't get along with your mother?"

"My father abandoned us when I was still a baby. My mother never remarried -- who'd have her? All through our childhood, she beat my brother Sam and me. She hit us with belts and her open hand in several drunken rages. She's been in and out of detox centers a hundred times. When Sam was one, and she couldn't get him to stop crying, she tried to suffocate him. Our father had to pull her off my brother before she killed him."

By now I was convinced I was on the right track.

"Since Thanksgiving or Christmas, she's been talking about coming into a lot of money. About how then she'll be able to invest and make herself rich."

"Any idea where all this money might come from?" I asked.

"The only place it *could* -- inherit it from Meemaw."

"Do you know if your mother's the first beneficiary of your grandmother's will?"

"She is. She'll inherit it all if Meemaw dies."

That was a motive for the attempted-murder last night. But still not enough evidence. "Has she attacked your grandmother before?"

"Not like -- like *this,* but she has flown at her in the past."

"If I *can* prove your mother tried to kill your grandmother, Mrs. Carter can refuse to prosecute."

"You can't *make* her?"

"If she died, of course, I could go forward. But if she's alive, she can refuse to prosecute and that would be the end of it."

"Despite all the fights, my Meemaw still loves my mother. She *might* not want to send her to jail."

"If she stays free, however, the next time she *might* kill Mrs. Carter."

"I know."

"Would you be willing to take a polygraph?"

"I have no problem with that. Will you ask my

mother if *she'll* take one?"

"That's exactly what I plan to do when I see her."

As I was leaving, the head nurse called to me from her station.

"Mrs. Carter told me this afternoon that she didn't want to be left alone with her daughter, the one we had to call Security on today. She's afraid of her own daughter."

"What about Security?"

"Well, we've been keeping an eye on Mrs. Carter's visitors, ever since her social worker made it clear to us that she suspects parent abuse in the case. When Mrs. Carter's daughter came today she was drunk and loud and acting *very* belligerent. I had to call Security and have her removed from the building."

****

There was no sign of forced entry into the

Carter house. Only four people had keys: the victim, her attendant Ruth who had already told me she would take a polygraph, the daughter Deidra, and Sara Cook, an old friend of the victim's.

After leaving Piedmont Hospital, I swung by Mrs. Cook's house in Buckhead. She was as elderly as her friend, so she could not have assaulted Mrs. Carter.

"Are you sure you still have your key, ma'am? Can I see it, just to make sure someone hasn't stolen it?"

"Why, sure, Detective," she said, and I sat by as she dug her arthritic fingers through an old cigar box. "Here it is!" she gladly proclaimed, holding up a key between two fingertips.

Taking it, I saw adhesive tape sticking to it. The words written on it were: GRACIE CARTER'S HOUSE KEY.

****

Ruth seemed to like phoning me and telling me the latest skullduggery at the Carter estate. "Detective Cartwright, I didn't want to tell you this when Deidra was around to hear. She told me a few days ago that if anything came in the mail for her mother from the bank, to take it and not tell her mother but give it straight to Deidra."

"Do you know *which* bank?"

I wrote the name down, intending to call a Georgia Federal bank investigator and see if this was my missing evidence.

Before I could make the call, Karen called me crying. "I just found out my mother is trying to get Meemaw put in a home against her will. Can my mother do that?"

"No," I assured her. "Your mother can't be forced into an institution while her mind's as healthy as it is."

"Have you asked my mother to take a polygraph yet?"

"I can't find her."

When I got through to the bank investigator, I told him about the case and requested he check my victim's account for any irregularities. He said he would call me when he found something.

Hanging up, the phone immediately rang. It was Ruth again. She whispered: "Deidra just showed up at Miz Carter's house. She's stinkin' drunk."

"I'm on my way, Ruth."

****

Ruth met me at the back door and led me into the living room. Deidra was passed out on the sofa. Both Ruth and I shook her, calling her name, until at last she came out of it.

Jumping to her feet, she walked quickly, limping grotesquely on only one high heel. "Summy stole my godamned shoe!" she exclaimed, although the other shoe was on the floor beside the sofa. She was extremely intoxicated and I almost couldn't understand her words.

When I asked if she would take a polygraph test she became enraged. "Get out of my house! Get out of my house!" Or words to the effect.

Ruth slipped out of the house with me. As we stood in the dark backyard, Deidra's tirade inside the house raged like a beast out of hell.

"You know how you told me to try and remember *any*thing suspicious Deidra might have said?" Ruth asked.

"Yes, Ruth?"

"I recall how, on Tuesday afternoon, the day Miz Carter was beat, that Deidra ax me if I was going to church that night. I said I was. She ax when was I leaving and I said a little after seven. She ax `What time are you going to get back?' and I said `Around eight-forty-five, as usual.' "

****

Back at the Homicide office, I had two calls. Both were pretty much the same, although one was from Deidra's son and the other from her past employer. Both said she was desperate for money.

****

The next afternoon, my first phone call was from the bank investigator. "I think you need to come to my office. I have a document you might be interested in."

****

On Saturday, April 19, three days before the near-fatal attack on her mother, Deidra Zenda entered the Georgia Federal bank in the Ansley Mall shopping center.

She handed the teller the letter which the bank investigator turned over to me. The letter, signed Grace Carter, stated that she wanted to change the names on a $15, 223.78 certificate of deposit. She wanted the names of Karen, Sam, and their other brother to be replaced with their mother's name, leaving her and Mrs. Carter as the sole co-owners of the CD. In case of Mrs. Carter's death, Deidra could cash the entire amount.

Taking this document to Mrs. Carter at Piedmont Hospital, she read it incredulously with her good eye.

"It's a forgery!" she exclaimed. "I would never take this money from my grandchildren!"

"Mrs. Carter," I said as gently as I could. "I believe Deidra is the one who tried to kill you. She did it so that she could get this CD."

"Oh, Lord!" She gasped, dropping her hand, and the bank document, to her side in the bed. "I just can't believe she would do that!" she wailed, although I detected doubt in her voice.

"Are you willing to let me arrest Deidra, Mrs. Carter?"

"For the CD, but not for the attack. I still don't think even *Deidra* would do that to *me*!"

The teller who had taken this forged letter remembered the gray-and-red-haired woman well.

"She was very agitated, and she had reacted angrily to a customer who was smoking in the line."

When I interviewed Deidra, she admitted passing the letter after I told her the teller described her, even remembered her argument with the smoker.

"Your mother says she did not sign that letter, Mrs. Zenda," I told her firmly.

"Of course my mother signed it. Don't you see her name there?"

"I see a signature that *resembles* your mother's, but I also see that whoever forged this bared down with the pen with more strength than your mother has possessed in *years.*"

"No. No, you're wrong." She wasn't drunk today, I noticed, and she wasn't going to break under questioning.

"When did she sign this, then, Mrs. Zenda?"

"I don't recall, but it was probably the day before I took it to the bank."

"Who typed the letter?"

"Well, I guess I typed it and my mother signed it."

"She tells me she would never drop her grand kids -- your own children -- from this CD."

"Well, it was my mother's idea to do it."

"To drop her grand kids' names and substitute yours?"

"My mother -- my mother loves me."

"Hopefully not as much as you `love' her."

"What's that supposed to mean?"

"I'm sending this document to the state crime lab. You remember we talked about all the great things the crime lab can do."

Standing, Deidra declared: "The next time you talk to *me*, you better have a warrant."

"I just might have one, Deidra," I said as she slammed the door behind her.

****

On May 13, after getting the results from the

crime lab that Mrs. Carter's name had been forged, I went to Deidra's home in nearby Dekalb County. I had a warrant, just as she had predicted.

Interviewing her in the Homicide office, she still denied everything.

"Then, how do you explain your mother's forged name on the document that you already admitted passing at the bank?"

"I don't know how it could have gotten on there."

"You're something else, Deidra. Real mother-of-the-year material. Not only do you forge a letter to take money away from your children, you have the indecency to try to kill your own mother! That's why the dog didn't bark that night, Deidra, because *it knows you*. It probably ran away from you like I saw it do the night you arrived when I was there. The reason you threw the pillow case over her head was so you wouldn't have to look into her face as you *killed her!"*

Unflappable, Deidra answered: "I was shopping

at Lenox Square when my mother was attacked."

"Who saw you?"

"I was alone. I was shopping for a mother's day present."

"A *month* before mother's day? What did you buy her, Deidra?"

"I couldn't find anything I thought she'd like."

I would later ask Karen how plausible this alibi was, and Karen would tell me her mother hadn't purchased Mrs. Carter any mother's day gift the year before. "I've never known of my mother to buy *any* gifts in advance," Karen told me. "She's the type that buys something on the way to the person's house."

****

Since the invalid could not come to court, I used an affidavit from Mrs. Carter where she swore the letter to the bank was a forgery. The municipal court judge bound the forgery charge over to the Fulton County grand jury.

Realizing I had a circumstantial case against Deidra for the assault on her mother, I constructed a large investigatory package for the District Attorney, requesting she also be indicted for the attack.

Before the DA could make a decision, Deidra called me. Smugly, she said, "My mother wants to speak to you, Detective Cartwright."

Mrs. Carter's voice came over the line. "I want to drop all charges against Deidra, Detective Cartwright."

I was shocked. "She tried to steal from you, Mrs. Carter. She tried to *kill* you!"

"I know," the old lady said sadly. "But we're family and she's begged me to forgive her. And I have. I don't want to prosecute my daughter."

"What if she tries to kill you again?"

"She won't."

So there never was an indictment.

Ruth continued to call me on an irregular basis for a few years, usually on holidays, telling me what was going on with the family and wishing me the season's greetings.

Her last call was more serious. "Deidra killed herself last night."

"Oh, yeah? I would never expect that from *her.*"

"Dekalb County poelease found her in her house. She shot herself. I guess even she couldn't live with what she had done."

Ruth didn't call any more after that. I often rode by the house on the hill in Morningside. A few years after this case, when I had been transferred from Homicide to the Burglary squad, I saw a for sale sign on Mrs. Carter's lawn. The house on the hill stood vacant, so I assumed the elderly lady was dead. I felt sure she'd taken care of her grand kids in her will. And Ruth.

MILLION DOLLAR ORDER.

Manuel's is literally a corner bar. The Maloofs have run it since 1956, which, ironically, is also when I was born. The second generation took over the business, although Manuel himself, a retired Dekalb County commissioner, often hobbled his massive body through, especially when ex-President Jimmy Carter, or other politicians, visited.

Celebrities, when in town shooting a movie, usually came by for a drink. It□ was a talking bar, except in the lower room where a juke box fat with diverse music, and a big-screen TV, could be found.

We cops usually congregated at the long, dark-brown bar. Or, when there was a crowd of us, we assembled around one of the party-tables in the upper barroom. Above this table were pictures of the Homicide squad and a plaque that read ZONE 7. That's an inside APD joke. In addition to the city's six patrol zones, Manuel's was the unofficial seventh precinct.

Above the cash register behind the bar, a photo of four stern-faced Red Dog cops glowered, looking hypergonadal. Dressed in black fatigues, Red Dog was the most feared squad we had. Their main objective was to leap out of unmarked vans and chase down street-corner drug dealers.

As you entered the men's room, you passed under a brown sheriff's deputy shirt. Its owner, Steve Pittard, died from natural causes. Steve was an old-time Manuelite.

It was Saturday night at Manuel's and the staff and several patrons watched one of the five mounted TV sets, anxiously awaiting the numbers in the state lottery.

Bill McCloskey, the head bartender who looked like a bearded lumberjack, quickly scribbled the winning numbers onto the only paper within reach, an order book.

Showing me the list of numbers, he was chortling. "You know, all our food orders are in numbers, just like this. Last Saturday I wrote down the winning lottery numbers for the cooks and left it in the order window. When I came back there were six plates of food there that nobody ordered! I forgot to tell them it was just the lottery numbers!"

MIDNIGHT OF THE SOUL.

When I was transferred to morning watch Homicide on September 30, 1986, it was like my world was turned upside-down.

The midnight-to-eight shift kills your sleeping pattern. It's the time the nuts come out, as I wrote about in the following story; while a cop I also did freelance writing.

****

I was a newspaper reporter when I encountered my first suicide scene.

The East Point cops let me inside the lady's apartment because they knew I'd applied to become a cop, so I got to see more than a reporter was usually allowed.

I don't recall her name, which seems fitting. She died alone, with her only love and companion, a gray tom cat.

When I entered her small, tidy apartment, the middle-aged woman was in a green armchair. Three buttons on her blouse were undone, revealing a blood-encrusted wound to her heart. Big, dark flies buzzed in the putrid summer air. Her windows were painted black with the night.

"Women almost always shoot themselves in the heart," the detective told me, like a vet to a rookie, his voice tempered by years of liquor and Marlboros.

"Vain to the very end. Don't want to disturb their looks," the other detective, Bob Matthews, told me.

She'd left a suicide note on her breakfast table, next to a half-eaten box of Rice Crispies. Her husband had been dead two years and she was very lonely. No kids. Only her cat, who she wanted the cops to give to a neighbor. The final blow to her weak grasp of life: she'd just been diagnosed with cancer.

"Anytime you get what *looks* like a suicide," Matthews told me over his shoulder as he examined the body, "and you don't find one of these," and he pointed to a bullet hole in the living room wall, "then you probably have a murder. Not a suicide."

"Is this where the bullet passed through her body?" I, the pre-rookie, nineteen years-old, asked.

"Nope. It's a hesitation shot. Suicides almost always do that. Maybe it's to test-fire the gun before they turn it on themselves. Don't ask me why. Maybe they do it to build up their nerve."

What psychic snake crawls into these peoples☐ minds? Suicides in Fulton County usually averaged 85 to 90 a year. When depression leads to thoughts of taking one's own life, it can be the most isolated feeling in the world. The worst angst can usually be felt during the deepest night, the so-called hour of the wolf. When the rest of Atlanta is either sleeping or partying, the afflicted struggle more strongly with their personal demons.

"Evenings for us are always busy," said Hal Goodloe, a tall, lanky counselor of the Fulton County Mental Health Emergency hotline for 16 years. Known as Buddy to his friends, the 44-year-old was a Decatur native where he lived with his wife and two kids. Buddy was a friend of mine. Over beers at Manuel's we often discussed books and our interest in the supernatural.

"During the daylight hours we get several calls from family members of the mentally ill. But on the morning watch, especially from 1:30 A.M. till 6:30, we mostly get calls from the people themselves who have problems."

Buddy worked the suicide hotline on the morning watch. His three-room office was on the street level of the one-block edifice called the Taj Mahal, the Fulton County Services building on Pryor Street across from the county court house. Usually a bright and bustling place during the day, on the morning watch Buddy was almost totally alone. The Fulton County Police 911 office was on the third floor. When Buddy clocked in at midnight, the building was dark and spooky. He could hear every noise the building made as he and his partner manned the phone lines like a non-broadcast version of call-in show

"Someone calling here at 4:00 A.M. has different problems than someone who calls at four in the afternoon. The afternoon shift gets many calls from other mental health agencies. My shift mostly gets the mentally ill person calling."

During lulls between calls, Buddy, a daytime denizen of the old Oxford Books, may catch up on some reading. But then the phone rings and it's another agonized soul with the black dog nipping at his or her heels.

"I've had a gun or two go off on the phone, but I don't know of anybody who's actually killed themselves while on the phone with us. If they say they've got a weapon, I tell them `I'll go on talking to you, but you've got to put the gun up. I don't want you shooting yourself while talking to me." In those cases there's an edge to their voice. You can hear them pouring pills out on the table, or hear a heavy object go thud and they'll tell you it's a gun.

"Just talking to a person may get them through another night, like convincing them to flush some pills. We may be helping them in tiny increments."

When I worked Homicide on the morning watch, I got to meet some of these agonized people who called Buddy in his steel-reinforced cave.

Some of the ones I met hadn't survived their dance with Thanatos. One despondent man threw himself onto the hot rail at the MARTA Midtown train station, sailing two stories from the dusty ledge above. Another tried to shoot himself in the head with a shotgun, but pulled away at the last second, literally blowing his face off but surviving his horrible wound for three days.

Can this dose of hemlock be better than living for them? Is Dr. Death their *only* fate?

The hotline averaged fifteen calls a night on the morning watch. "My watch got 1,100 calls the first quarter of this year," said Buddy. "Forty-six percent were suicide calls, 29 percent alcohol and drugs, and 24 percent were persons out of control. Eighty percent of the calls on my watch are anonymous."

Buddy could tell you his hours weren't for everyone. "There's a lot of stress listening to human tragedy. To avoid total burnout, you have to leave your work at the office. Try not to think about what happened last night. Some social workers become hermits, but that's not the thing to do. I seek activities during the day." Such as watching Mystery Science Theater 3000 with his kids. He also haunted Oxford Books on Pharr Road, seeking psych books, mysteries, true crime.

His work partner, Robert Zachary, spent his

daylight hours cleaning out old buildings, looking for rare books and relics. He'd found several forgotten treasures in moldy basements and attics, some more than a hundred years old, and he sold them at antique shows.

They needed the escape to deal with the nightly calls from depressives. "Depression and suicide are prevalent in the middle of the night," said Buddy. "Recently I've gotten a lot of crack addicts calling from pay phones around four. Usually they say they're about to kill themselves. They're out of money. They've been stealing from their family and friends, so they have no one to turn to but us."

Many callers felt isolated. "One of the things I tell them is you have to stop staying up all night and sleeping the day away. They get out of sync with everyone else. That's incredibly lonely. Just them and their problems. Isolation is not good, and there's a direct correlation between that and depression. Isolation can lead to suicidal feelings, especially late on a gloomy night. Depression plus isolation plus sleepiness equals suicidal feelings. That makes our phones ring."

It was so quiet when Buddy got these calls, sometimes he could hear crickets and birds over the phone, or, like recently, the creaky lament of a porch swing slowly rocking back and forth as the caller cried.

Stuck in his tiny office, Buddy could identify with feelings of isolation. To go to the restroom at work he must walk down a shadowy corridor, past dark, locked office doors. He could hear the pop of every concealed pipe in the building. The silence was huge. You tended to lower your voice when speaking with him, like talking during church.

There was a security guard outside, his metal chair tipped against the marble facade of the Taj Mahal. "It's usually calm and peaceful during these hours," he said. "That's how I like it." He cocked his head at the sound of a distant siren.

The siren could be an ambulance going to a suicide scene, and I'm reminded of my first suicide crime scene, and the countless others I've seen as a cop. That woman in East Point had gone through her house and pinned paper notes to all her possessions, with requests for distributing them to the living. I wondered what she thought as she prepared those notes, then went for the pistol. Her fragile life, it seemed, was like petals falling one by one from a flower until it was gone.

"My eyes start drooping around five to six," said Buddy. "Then around the last hour I revive." It was like that when I worked morning watch Homicide. I could be dog-tired, but I became energized seeing the pink rays of the dawning sun crawling slowly down from the tallest Midtown tower; or by the smell of hot coffee pushed my way by a sleepy-eyed waitress at the IHOP next to the Jewish Community Center on Peachtree. With the arrival of dawn, the nocturnal demons receded to their netherworld.

"The MARTA bus traffic picks up around six," Buddy said. "The whole city's starting to awake. All the busses kind of make the building tremble. I can see the little guy from the cafeteria across the street arrive and open shop."

The day watch shift arrived early that morning so that Buddy could move his car. Tonight he parked in the reserved space for the police chief. "You can do that on my shift," he said. "When I arrive, the parking lot's empty."

Buddy drove carefreely out of town as everyone else was driving in. But there are only so many hours in a day. When the darkness returned, so would Buddy and I and all the other creatures of the night.

TESTIMONY FROM A GHOST.

The two doctors never stopped working on the wounded young woman although I could tell by their expressions they knew *I* was not a real medico. I was dressed in scrubs, standing at the table in the Grady Emergency Operating Room as they were preparing to anesthetize my victim.

The docs hadn't challenged me, but I saw the head nurse running my way, hurling obscenities. She looked lots meaner than Nurse Ratchet. "Who the fucking hell are *you* and how the fucking hell did you get in here?" she screeched.

"I'm the Homicide detective working this case," I told her, then lowered my voice so Rebecca couldn't hear. "They told me in the ER she's not expected to live. I *had* to speak to her before it was too late."

"I don't give a flying fuck if you *are* the Homicide detective -- you don't belong in *here!* Now get out!"

But it was all right. Rebecca Hall had already told me who shot her and her friend Helene Zellner. Helene couldn't tell me. She was already dead.

****

Only four days before Christmas. Around one in the morning of the twenty-first, 1986, renters in the modest apartments across from the Springdale Nursing Home heard gunshots. Witnesses would later report looking out the window and seeing activity in the driveway of the Home. Under a street light, they saw a small car parked, two men standing outside it when one opened fire with a handgun and a young woman fell from the car. The gunman stood above her as she rolled on the pavement, trying in vain to avoid the bullets.

The cops were called as the two men ran down the street.

Zone 3 officers converged quickly, finding a dead woman sitting in the bullet-riddled car, holding a squalling infant in her blood-soaked lap.

The second young woman lay in the parking lot on her back, in shock and barely alive.

"Start a four code three!" a young officer radioed to his dispatcher. "And start Homicide!"

****

I noted the time was 1:30 when I rolled on the call on Atlanta's southside, near its border with East Point. The sky was cloudy but, luckily, there was no rain to disturb the outside crime scene. As I drove, I sipped coffee from a Styrofoam cup, burning my lips.

A fire rescue truck mingled its flashing red beacons with the blue lights on half a dozen police cruisers.

"Your forty-eight's in that car," a uniform told me, directing the beam of his flashlight to a blue Chevette parked with its motor off in the horse-shoe-shaped drive. "A second victim, a black female, has been taken to Grady low-sick."

I was always a little sleepy on the morning watch, but this whodunit, and all the coffee I'd swilled, made my heart start tapping.

Going to the Chevette, I looked first at the ignition. It was empty. Swirling my flashlight around the interior, I spotted a key ring attached to a green disk lying in the drivers-side floorboard. In the passenger's seat was Helene Zellner [I've changed her last name], a hefty white female wearing an open green jacket, blue jeans, and white slip-on shoes. Her right hand was wedged between her legs and she slumped toward the driver's seat with her left arm draped across the driver's side of the gear-shifter. The passenger-side door window was completely shattered, as if one or more bullets had been fired through it.

Stretching rubber gloves over my long fingers, I reached through the shattered window and felt the victim was still warm. In the dark, I saw no blood on her.

A baby bag was in the back seat, sprayed with shattered glass.

"The victim had a baby in her lap when I arrived," Officer R. L. Holder told me, peering over my shoulder. "A nurse from the Home here came and took the baby. It's been transported to Grady."

A burgundy jacket lay on the tarmac a few feet from the car. "That's where we found the second victim," Holder said.

Examining the area around the jacket, I found a flattened bullet slug and a pack of Kools. There were still cigarettes in it, so I confiscated this for later analysis.

With an ID tech, the crime scene was thoroughly photographed.

I said to a rookie standing near by: "Put on some gloves. I need you to help me remove the body."

"You're kidding -- right?" he said. "I thought the EMTs removed bodies."

"I need to pull her out of the car so I can examine the wounds."

His expression told me he wanted nothing to do with touching dead bodies, but his fellow officers, veterans unlike him, were watching. He donned the gloves and helped me pull the twenty-six-year-old from the car and lay her on the pavement.

Looking under the victim's blouse, I could see no wounds. "You gotta do that?" the rook muttered.

"I gotta do this," I said, turning the body onto her front and examining her back. Along her mid-back, next to her spine, was a bullet wound.

****

The zone guys helped canvas the neighborhood for witnesses. I found employees inside the nursing home who reported hearing two shots, a pause, then two or three more reports.

Neighbors also reported hearing shots. The neighbors, and also nursing home employees, as well as some elderly residents, looked out their windows. From a distance, they all saw two men. No one was close enough to see their faces.

"I'm going to need the survivor's account," I told Officer Holder. "I'm through here at the crime scene. I'm going to Grady."

****

It was around 3:30 when I rolled into the ER. Things were slow and a sleepiness seemed to hang in the air.

"Sterling -- the two-month-old infant -- checked out fine," a cheery ER nurse told me. "But the adult female's not expected to pull through."

"Where is she?"

"She's already been taken up to the Emergency OR."

Not a good sign. If she died, I realized, it would be almost impossible to get an ID on the two men the other witnesses reported seeing.

Riding the elevator to the third floor, I asked a scurrying nurse where the black female gunshot victim was.

"She's already in OR," she replied, and was gone.

That posed a dilemma. What if she died in

there?

A doctor and a nurse walked into a room and I followed. This was a lounge and they doffed their green scrubs and stuffed them into a barrel.

Another doctor, in street clothes, came in and took scrubs from a drawer and climbed into them. There were even scrubs for the shoes.

That gave me an idea. Taking off my jacket and tossing it onto a sofa, I dressed in scrubs, too. The .38 in my shoulder holster made a bulge that the others didn't have.

Finding my way into the surgical arena, I went to the table under the big lamps where the twenty-one-year-old black female was being prepped for emergency surgery. I knew I couldn't waste time. Leaning over her, I said: "Rebecca. Who shot you and Helene?"

A doctor, looking oddly at me, returned to cleaning one of the three bleeding wounds.

Rebecca, writhing in pain, said: "Jack."

"Why did he shoot you?"

"Jack's a friend of Chris. Helene just had a baby by Chris."

"Sterling?"

"Mm-hmm. The baby's real sick. Helene asked me to drive her, to find Chris, to ask him to please give her some money to help pay some of the medical bills. We found Chris, he was with Jack. Chris argued with Helene, then he told Jack to `burn her, burn her.' That's when -- *oh!* -- Jack shot Helene. Then he came after me. That hurts!"

"I know it does, Rebecca. Just a few more questions."

"I want to tell you, to help you. After Jack killed Helene, Chris told him he had to kill me, too, because I had seen him kill Helene. That's when -- *oh!* -- Jack came after me. He shot me once in the car, then I tried to get away, but I fell and I was rolling on the ground and he was just standing over me shooting."

The viciousness of the attack stunned me like a slap. The doctors kept working, not saying a word.

"Do you know their last names, Rebecca?"

"No. I just know Chris is the baby's daddy. Helene covered the baby with her body when Jack started shooting." She gritted her teeth in pain, then kept talking. "Chris is on probation for drugs. Helene threatened to sue him for child support. That's what started the argument."

That's when the head nurse barged in and made me leave.

****

Despite the predictions, Rebecca did not die. In fact, the next day I came in early and interviewed her in her hospital room. She was alert and in some pain, but she was able to supply more details than she had in the OR.

"Helene was crying because she said the baby was real sick and was gonna die," the petite Rebecca continued. She was a sweet person and I wondered whether her murdered friend was, also. "I let Helene stay with me, at my apartment. I drove her around looking for Chris. We found him at Jack's apartment.

Chris and Helene had another argument there and she stormed out. In the parking lot, she kicked Chris' car, but I don't think she hurt it.

"I pulled into the nursing home parking lot and turned off the engine. Helene was sitting in the passenger seat, with Sterling in her lap, when Chris walked up and knocked on Helene's window. He told her to give him Sterling, that he would take Sterling to Grady himself. Helene was still crying, and she said `No.' She'd rolled her window down halfway, and then she said `I'm not gonna argue with you anymore,' and started rolling the window back up.

"Jack was with Chris, and I heard Chris say to Jack `Jack, go on burn her!' I *tried* to drive off, but Jack shot Helene twice through the window. After the first shot, Helene said `Oh no, the baby!' She fell over Sterling and I knew she was dead.

"I remember after Jack shot Helene, Chris said to him `You went too far! I didn't want you to kill her! Now you gotta kill *her,* 'meaning me, `'cause she seen everything.' When Jack came over to shoot me, I heard him say to Chris `You're in this with me.'

"Jack yanked open my door. I was trying to get my keys to turn, but they fell to the floor, and he shot me. He shot me in my chest and stomach. I fell out of the car and was rolling on the pavement. That must be when he shot me in my back.

"After the shooting, they ran across the street. They left me on the ground. I was waving my hand for someone to please help me."

Remembering the crime scene, where I found Rebecca's jacket and a pack of cigarettes, I asked, "Do you smoke Kools?"

"I don't smoke."

"What brand did Helene smoke?"

"Newports. Why? Is that important?"

"I think Jack dropped a pack of Kools while he was shooting you. His fingerprints might be on the cellophane."

After leaving Rebecca's room, I walked to the hospital security office on the ground floor. "I need to speak to a supervisor," I told the officer in the gray uniform shirt, working at a desk, who pointed with his pencil to a door.

"Sergeant Davis," I said, entering and reading his name plate. "I've got a murder witness who's been admitted." I wrote her name and room number on a piece of paper and handed it to the beefy man. "She's my only strong witness and both shooters are still at large."

"You want us to keep a guard outside her door?"

"That'd be great if you would. Just to be on the safe side."

****

Delivering a death notification is dreadful, but it comes with the territory.

Helene had a sister named Leona. Finding Leona in her working-class neighborhood, I showed her the driver's license I had taken from my victim's purse. "Yes, that's my sister," she said. I could tell by her green eyes, and the way she was arching her back as if distancing herself from me would soften the blow, that she already suspected the worst.

"I'm sorry to inform you, but your sister is dead."

Her tears flowed. "Who killed my sister?"

"My witness said it was her baby's father, Chris. Do you know Chris?"

"Oh, *yes.* I know the bastard."

"Do you know Chris' last name?"

"Mapp. Christopher Mapp. I always knew that dope-dealin' bastard would hurt Helene! I tried to warn her, she just would *not* listen!"

"So, they've argued before?"

"They've been fighting over paying Sterling's medical bills. He's seriously ill and might die. Chris has fired at Helene before."

"Oh, yeah?" I said, lifting my eyebrows.

"Helene kept the bullet casing. She even showed it to me. She said she would hold on to it as `evidence.' Helene was afraid Chris might kill her one day."

"Do you know Jack?"

"Yeah, that's his friend. They met when they were both serving time in Fort Leavenworth -- you know, the army prison?"

"Okay."

"Can you tell me where Sterling is?"

"He's at the children's shelter. Someone from there should be contacting you soon. Leona. Can you wait here while I see if our ID section has a photo of Chris Mapp?"

"Yes," she said, almost jovial.

Driving to headquarters Downtown, I checked out the suspect's mugshot. Returning to the Homicide office, both Leona and her boyfriend identified it as Christopher Mapp.

****

When I secured an arrest warrant for Mapp, it was covered by the local TV news and in the *Atlanta*

Journal and Constitution. It was a sensational murder story. It also prompted the twenty-six-year-old Mapp to call Homicide and say that he wanted to turn himself in.

****

On December 22, Mapp surrendered himself. I ushered the clean-cut young man into an interview room where I turned on a tape recorder. Miranda was the first thing on the tape.

Nervously, Mapp took out a pack of cigarettes and lit one. I noticed they were unfiltered Camels, not Kools like what I'd found at the crime scene.

Handing him a standard waiver of counsel form, I asked, "Can you read?"

"Yes."

"How far did you go in school?"

"I completed one year of college." He agreed to make a statement.

Mapp acknowledged that he and Helene had

been arguing. His friend Jack was with him. "And that Rebecca chick opened up her glove compartment and Jack he thought she had something in there and he started firing a pistol. I was telling him `Naw, naw.' But that psycho did the shooting and I couldn't stop him."

That differed from Rebecca's version.

"See, I didn't know that he was gonna kill them two women."

It took all my power not to look startled. "Why did Jack kill Rebecca?"

"I guess 'cause she seen what he did to Helene."

That meant Mapp thought Rebecca was dead. He didn't *know* I had a witness who could tear his story apart. I didn't betray this secret.

"Do you admit Sterling is your son?"

"That's what Helene said. That I was. We lived together a few months, you know."

"What's Jack's real name?"

"Lynn Jackson."

"Did you hear him say anything prior to his --
killing these two women?"

"I heard him say he was gonna burn 'em."

I copied into my notes that Rebecca said Mapp
had been the one who said to "burn" them. "Chris,
did you in any way tell Lynn Jackson to shoot Helene
or Rebecca?"

He licked his lips nervously, avoiding my eyes.
His hands were clasped firmly at stomach level. "I
must say that I was talking but I did not tell him to
hurt them in any way."

"Do you have a gun?"

"No."

"Have you *ever* shot at Helene?"

"No." I didn't mention this to Mapp, but
Helene's sister, earlier that day had given me the .38
casing she said Helene carried around as her
"evidence."

"Where is the murder weapon now?"

"I don't know. It's Jack's gun. And, man, Jack's
been calling and calling me, saying we gotta get

together about this thing."

"He's been calling you, huh? Would you agree to us recording you talking to Jackson on the phone?"

"I'll do it. I will."

****

"We need to get the shooter," said the Homicide lieutenant, a tall black man who, among ourselves, we called Hollywood because of his apparent love of starring in press conferences. As usual, his suit looked tailor-made, standing in direct contrast to my hopelessly unkempt attire.

Based on Mapp's statement, I secured an arrest warrant for Lynn Jackson for the murder of Helene Zellner. Not only did we need to snatch up "Jack," but I also wanted better evidence to take to court.

"For us to record Jackson talking on the telephone to Mapp," Hollywood said to me as he sat behind his enlarged desk, "we need to let him go home."

"That'll be risky," I said. "What if he runs?"

"I'll send him home with a black detective from Fugitive. That way it won't cause attention in his neighborhood."

Watching Detective Buster Edmonson drive off with Mapp, I began a nerve-wracking waiting game.

Back at my desk in a small room in the front of the Homicide office, I called Southern Bell Security and arranged a trace to be put on Mapp's phone.

Smoking too many cigarettes, I waited. By midnight, Buster returned with Mapp to the Homicide office.

"The bastard never called," Buster said.

****

Mapp phoned me the next day.

"Jack just called me. He said he's hiding out in Fort Gaines, Florida."

"We've got to lure him back to Atlanta, Chris."

"I know. I told him to get back up here, hook up with me 'cause I've got a thousand dollars and a van. I told him we could leave Georgia, sleep in the van and not have to rent motel rooms."

"Did he buy it?"

"He bought it. Jack said he'd call me at home tomorrow when he got back in town."

Tomorrow was Christmas Eve.

****

Even cops -- though obviously not all of us -- get to take Christmas off. On the twenty-fourth, as I tried to arrange a UC team, I found that all of them were off.

"This is what I need for you to do," I told Officer Singleterry. "Our guy has already told me he's going to be with his girlfriend in his burgundy Cadillac. When the shooter arrives, they're going to leave 616 Kennedy Street. I need a black officer in plainclothes to watch that house. Since I can't get any UC cops, you'll have to do it with your uniform shirt off."

The Zone 5 officer agreed, although he realized he'd have to stand outside in the freezing cold in his v-neck tee-shirt. At the last minute we were able to scare up a UC car from Internal Affairs. I knew our fleet of detective cars looked like cop cars -- and I didn't want to scare off our shooter.

"I'll have two marked zone units with me," I told Singleterry. "We'll be hiding a few blocks away from you. When you spot Mapp's Caddie, radio for us and we'll snatch their asses up. Okay?"

"Let's do it to it."

****

Stakeouts. I *hate* stakeouts.

Waiting, waiting, waiting with nothing else to do. After we'd been sitting out for a few hours, I could tell the two uniforms behind me were getting bored. I walked back to them, intending to keep up their spirits with a pep talk.

The uniform guys killed time by discussing the latest zone gossip, and football scores, but now I could tell they were growing restless with all this inaction.

"You think your shooter's not gonna show, Cartwright?" one of them asked.

"They're moving," Singleterry suddenly radioed. We scrambled for our cars. "They just drove up Kennedy Street, turning onto Northside Drive." Our adrenaline started to pump.

The white zone cars passed me on the street, flying along with their blue lights warning the light holiday traffic. We were ready to take care of business -- at last.

"Turning onto Martin Luther King Drive," Singleterry radioed, and I noticed a horde of other Zone 5 cars coming to assist. So many cop cars took down the Caddie that I had to park the length of a football field away and run up to assist.

It looked like a hundred cops had their black

.38s trained at the car where all three passengers had their arms pressed against the roof. Mapp's new girlfriend, who was in on the ruse, was driving. I saw Mapp in the front passenger seat. I recognized the black male in the back from his mugshot. Lynn Jackson!

Snatching each person out, frisking them and handcuffing them, I turned to one of the take-down officers and nodded once. He holstered his weapon and paced to his squad car. Leaning inside, he turned on a miniature tape recorder. We put Mapp and Jackson into the back of this car and left them alone. Since we hadn't gotten Jackson's confession on a phone call, I decided this would be our next best bet. Mapp had already been told about it.

Giving the two murder suspects time to talk, I acted as though I were searching Mapp's Caddie.

After that I decided they'd had enough time. "Go ahead and transport the two perps to Homicide," I told the uniform officer.

Once they were gone, I went to the squad car

where Mapp's girlfriend had been detained. "They're gone," I said, letting her out.

Officer Singleterry, our lookout man, joined us. Now wearing his heavy blue jacket, he was still shivering from the biting cold.

****

I let Jackson sit alone in the interrogation room. When finally I walked in and closed the door behind me, the twenty-five-year-old watched me with cold brown eyes. He looked scruffy and street, opposite of the almost-collegian look of his friend Mapp.

After Mirandizing him, I said, "Lynn Jackson, you're charged with the murder of Helene Zellner and Rebecca Hall." I still didn't want either of the perps to know my main witness was not really dead.

"I was at a party that night."

"*What* night? I didn't tell you any date!"

Obviously rattled by this, Jackson took out a

pack of Kools from his shirt pocket and lit one. That, I realized, explained where the pack of Kools at the crime scene had come from. Jackson must have dropped them while he was shooting Rebecca. Loose ends were starting to tie up nicely.

"I knew you'd say you were at a party."

He cocked an eyebrow my way.

I pulled the miniature tape recorder from my jacket pocket and laid it before me on the table. Jackson looked at it with widening eyes, trying to figure out what damage this Toshiba might do him.

After a theatrical pause, I hit the play button.

The first voice on the tape was me advising my two suspects of their rights under Miranda, then came the slam of the car door that left them alone.

Mapp, perhaps hamming it up *too* much, was audibly crying. Much of the conversation was unintelligible, but Jackson could be heard saying: "You know they waited till you came to your mother's house, you know that . . . I ain't done nothin' . . . homeboy. I ain't gonna say I did no shootin'. Now be quiet . . . Look. I ain't sayin' nothin' 'cause I don't know nothin' . . . An' *you* don't know nothin', right? . . . They ain't got nothin', homeboy. Don't you say nothin'. Tell 'em you don't know nothin'. Tell 'em me an' you was at a party . . . Only thing we'll tell 'em is that we know each other from the jail house, okay? . . . We were at a party that night, okay? . . . Homeboy, *please* don't tell 'em . . . Keep your mouth closed . . . I'm not the one they lookin' for. They lookin' for *you.* But I did the shootin'."

Mapp can be heard responding: "I know, man, but don't say nothin'."

"They ain't got nothin' on us, we was at a party that night. An' you know we got witnesses that can say we was at a party. Don't you say I did no shootin'. *Please,* homeboy. I ain't got nothin' to say. I ain't talkin' to nobody . . . "

Switching off the tape recorder, I could see a shocked look of disbelief on Jackson's face. His Kool had burned all the way down to his knuckles, but he seemed as though he couldn't move.

"You want to tell me *your* side of the story, Jack?" I asked, using his street name to show him I knew more about him than he thought I did.

He slowly got himself together. At last stuffing his cigarette butt down the empty Coke can he was using as an ashtray, he muttered, "I ain't got nothin' to tell you."

I ended the interview there.

****

In the prelim, I smiled smugly as Christopher Mapp testified about how his psycho partner killed these girls and he tried everything he could to stop him.

"I have a witness who can totally rebut that, your honor," I announced and Mapp's eyes snapped toward me.

"Call that witness, then," the judge ordered.

"She's in the corridor, your honor. I'll have to help her in."

When I helped the short, kind-looking Rebecca down the aisle, as she hobbled on crutches because of her wounds, I recall looking into the eyes of the two defendants and wishing that I had a camcorder. They really *thought* they were seeing a ghost, because I had never told them Rebecca had survived her attack.

Leaning on her crutches, Rebecca raised her right hand and the solicitor swore her in.

Her testimony at the later trial lacked the grand entrance it had at the prelim, but still it was strong evidence. Jackson decided to take the stand and say that he thought Rebecca was going for a gun, so he shot her in self-defense.

The defense attorney had requested the rule of sequestration, which meant that all witnesses, including me, had to wait outside the court room. My girlfriend at the time, however, watched from the audience and later related to me the cunning strategy that exposed Jackson's deceit.

The ADA, Carol Wahl, a tall blonde, asked

Jackson, "What hand did Ms. Hall use when she reached for what you're saying you thought was a gun?"

Grinding his teeth together for a moment, Jackson blurted: "Right. Her right hand."

Carol re-called Rebecca to the stand. Handing her a piece of paper and a pen, Carol asked: "Would you write your name on the paper, please?"

With her left hand, Rebecca took the pen and signed her name. Glancing with a smile at the jury, Carol asked Rebecca: "Are you left-handed, Ms. Hall?"

"Yes, I'm left-handed," she answered, not knowing the significance of the revelation.

Mapp hung his head and muttered.

The jury deliberated briefly before returning with a verdict of guilty against both defendants. The judge sentenced Mapp and Jackson to life for the murder of Helene and twenty-five years -- consecutively -- for the shooting of Rebecca.

Rebecca and the Zellner family were elated at

the sentences. "I feel so good," Rebecca said perkily, despite her painful wounds, as she left the superior court building. "Justice was done."

The jury had deliberated less than three hours.

MURDER IN A STRIP BAR.

The strippers had put their clothes on by the time we arrived at the seedy nude bar on the southside. It wasn't my case, I was just along to assist.

The place on Cleveland Ave had been converted from a Ponderosa steak house. The interior was redone in black paint and the place smelled of booze and overworked cheap perfume. Dancers and waitresses, dressed in colorful tights and velcro-snapped bikinis, sat at shadowed tables, smoking cigarettes and chatting, watching us work.

A man, who we at first suspected had

underworld connections, lay dead from a single gunshot wound. His lawyer had been with him. They were out celebrating New Year's Eve.

"I put my arm around his shoulder," the distraught man said, "and he just fell dead."

Was it some kind of mob hit? I even speculated if the lawyer's embrace was somehow connected to the shooting. A bullet hole was found in the front facade of the building. No one could have seen through the wall to aim at the victim. It was very perplexing.

The next day a sixty-four-year-old man entered the Homicide office, saying: "I want to confess to a murder last night." His shoulders slumped as did his head, and he sighed loud and often.

His incredible statement was taken. "It was New Year's Eve. I live in the apartments across from the titty bar. At midnight I just came outside with my pistol and fired some shots. You know, it was New Year's Eve and all."

One of his stray shots penetrated the facade of

the club and found its way into the chest of our victim, just as his lawyer embraced him.

THE BEAST SIGHTED.

Hearing the communal shout of the rioting mob, still three blocks from my position, and watching a hail of rocks and bottles fly, I was thinking: This is the beast. It is excreting rocks and bottles over us.

Every APD cop was in riot gear. All off-days canceled. A couple of white supremacists came here, the state capitol, to give a speech. They were met by thousands of black protesters who turned violent. The state patrol was helping us and the national guard was on standby.

My squad advanced to fight the beast. In its wake were overturned cars, looted stores, innocent victims savagely beaten.

Frenzy. Chaos. The beast.

The Hindu religion has statues of their various gods. The Hindus realize the statues aren't really gods, but an earthly representation of a cosmic force beyond our understanding.

In the same way these rioters are the beast, I think. The beast wants to devour us, to devour the sun and the stars.

The lust for destruction, the evilness of the beast, can be seen in smaller parts in the violence of the killer, the rapist, or the burglar who destroys your feeling of inner sanctum.

Suddenly cops aren't just doughnut-eating ticket-writers, I think sardonically, as my squad advances toward the rioters. Slipping over all the bricks and bottles in the closed-down street, gripping my riot baton tightly, my familiar breath fogging the visor of my helmet, I hear the beast growl again. But the beast is essentially a coward, and begins its retreat at our advance.

****

Sopping up after the worst of the riot was over, I gazed at all the bricks and rocks littering the dead Downtown streets and sidewalks.

It seemed that every glass storefront on Peachtree Street was shattered. Voices over the radio strapped to my gunbelt were calling about burglaries here and there. Under protection of the anarchy of the angry crowds, burglars and looters had gone wild. Now we were retaking Downtown, as I ducked through yet another shattered store window. Illuminating its ruined innards with my flashlight, I mused about chaos. Is order something most humans seek, disdaining bedlam?

The city was now calm, yet in the back of this dark store I heard the sound of people running. We caught three burglars hiding behind spilled racks of clothing. Pistol drawn, I yelled: "On the floor! On the floor!"

After handcuffing them, we led them back out to the street and loaded them into an already overstuffed paddy wagon.

Taking a quick smoke break, two other cops and I, were silent. Looking at all the rocks and bricks, I thought how much Downtown looked like the surface of the moon.

HOT DEATH.

A pedestrian that night heard a boom and looked across Ponce de Leon Avenue to see a human fireball race across the parking deck of the old Goodyear tire store. In horror, he watched the man leap off the edge and fly through the air like a shooting star.

Seeing a SWAT car moving up the street in the

11:30 P.M. traffic, he ran to alert them. He didn't see the man in the shadowy lot who dropped something that rolled under a flaming van before fleeing.

Officers Harvey and Devita pulled into the secluded lot where the van was now totally engulfed in flames. Locating the victim on the ground near Penn Avenue, Officer Harvey radioed: "Start me a four code three." The ambulance on the way with a rush priority, the cops gave what first aid they could. The fall from the deck had extinguished the flames but they could see he had extensive second and third degree burns and was barely conscious.

On July 30, 1987, I reported to the office just before midnight. My sarge told me to get down to the Grady ER.

There I found the victim already being treated in one of the rooms. The nurses and doctors were in great haste, and one of the doctors took me aside and whispered that the victim was not expected to live. I needed a dying declaration and the doctor knew it. "I don't believe in telling them they're terminal," the doctor protested. "It makes them lose hope."

"I may *need* it to make an arrest," I countered.

He compromised. Leaning over the semiconscious victim, who lay naked on the gurney, his clothes burned off, the physician told him: "We're trying to save your life." Hoping that would be legal enough, I moved over the man and asked what happened to him.

"J.P. set me on fire," he rasped, not able to open his eyes. I asked if he knew J.P.'s real name. "William Norris. Just got out of jail." I asked if he knew why Norris had done this. He shook his head negative. "Thrown something on me." A nurse then stuck a tube down the victim's throat, down to his stomach, and my interview was over.

When I stepped away from the gurney, a doctor whispered to me: "He won't live three days with these severe burns." This would become true.

All of his clothes had burned off, so we had no ID, but he'd given his name to the ambulance crew.

Greg Searcy. When I later ran a check on him, I found a colossal crime sheet and several aliases. He'd been arrested for burglary, auto theft, and robbery. At the time of this attack he was on probation that would expire in two years.

His history sheet listed him as single, born in Atlanta, and having five false front teeth.

While still in our ID section, I also had the techs run the name he'd given for his assailant. They found one William Norris and, like Searcy had said, Norris had just gotten out of city jail.

Norris was five years older than Searcy and had a rap sheet almost as bad. There had been robbery, theft, motor vehicle thefts and fighting. He had a scar over his right temple.

The fire department had extinguished the flaming van by the time I arrived around 1:00 A.M. The parking lot was in the rear of the repair bays. Zone 2 Officer Brooker Wolfe was securing the crime scene and keeping back the small crowd of curiosity seekers. Prodding the ruined van with a fingertip, a clip board wedged under one arm, was Lt. J. E. Williams of the fire department's Arson squad.

"The fire started in the interior, as opposed to the engine," Williams told me as I joined him. Looking into the reeking van I could smell gasoline. "I'd say it might have started in the front passenger seat and spread to the rear. And look at this."

With his flashlight, he showed me something odd on the pavement. At first I thought it was the sole of a shoe. But it wasn't.

"It's the sole of the victim's *foot,*" Williams told me. In the heat it had pulled off like a bedroom slipper, fusing onto the concrete.

With our flashlights, we could follow the victim's charred route from the van. As he ran burning, the contents of his pockets fell to the parking deck. I noted an Afro comb, and a *Jet* magazine further along. Then he ran into a parked car so hard he dented the trunk. Then to the edge of the high deck and below, the disturbed weeds where he landed.

"Hell of a way to get it," I muttered and Williams nodded grimly.

Now we had good suspicion gas was used to ignite the van and our victim. I went to Officer Wolfe and requested he check any open gas stations in the area for someone without a car buying a small amount of gas. He was back in less than ten minutes.

"Two blocks away at the Gulf station on Ponce," Wolfe told me. "They sold a small amount of gas to a black male some time before midnight."

Going there, I spoke with the two nighttime attendants. "He came in and said his car wasn't getting gas to the carburetor. He needed a little bit to get it started. He had a Schlitz Malt liquor can he wanted to pump it into." Instead, they gave him an antifreeze jug and asked how much he wanted. He pulled seventy-six cents from the pocket of his tattered clothes but only pumped forty-two cents before walking east on Ponce. Toward the Goodyear store.

I confiscated the register tape which put the

time of purchase at 11:05 P.M..

Returning to the crime scene, we found beneath the van a charred Atlas antifreeze jug. Atlas was the exclusive brand sold by Gulf. The ID tech attempted to lift latents with negative results.

The crime scene was extensively photographed by the tech, and precise measurements taken. Returning to the ID section at police headquarters on Decatur Street Downtown, I checked out the suspect's mug shot. Putting it in with other mug shots, I had the Gulf attendants view them. One said he thought the photo of Norris was the guy they'd sold the gas to. The other attendant wasn't sure, saying he'd have to see him in person.

That area of Ponce was overflowing with homeless people. As a patrolman, this had been my beat, so I knew several people out there. It was them I sought for more evidence.

Around 5:00 A.M. one of my snitches told me what he had heard happened in that van in the back deck. "I seen J. P. a few hours ago an' he told me he burned Slim." Slim was Searcy's street name. "They had stole a bike together about a month ago, supposed to split the money, but Slim kept *all* the money then *bragged* about not givin' J. P. his share. That pissed - off J. P. He found Slim tonight sleepin' in a empty labor pool van behind the tire store. J. P. got some gas in a can an' threw it on Slim, then woke him up holdin' matches in his hand, sayin' he was gonna burn Slim. Slim just laughed at him and called him a punk."

I already knew the rest.

By this time all the street people I spoke to on Ponce de Leon already knew that "J. P. burned Slim." Only, nobody knew where Norris was hiding. I chased several sightings down, but by dawn Norris was still out there somewhere.

At 8:00 A.M. I got an arrest warrant for Norris. As the victim was still alive at the time, the charge was aggravated battery. I created a BOLO flyer and put it in the interdepartmental mail for the zones and other squads. Before going home to try to sleep, I broadcast the lookout for Norris over the police zones.

****

Coming in early that evening, I went to the Grady Burn unit. When I entered the ward a sick odor similar to barbecue assaulted my nose. Everything was deathly quiet: no radios or televisions, no chatter from visitors. Walking by each open door, I saw weird tableaus inside the shadowy rooms: motionless victims wrapped like mummies, several with arms and legs in traction in what seemed painful and unnatural positions, like grotesque ballet dancers frozen in time. Everyone was sedated, including Searcy, but his attending nurse said he thought Searcy could probably look at the mug shots I carried. "You know it isn't the wounds that kill these burn victims," the nurse told me. "It's the infection that almost invariably sets in."

Searcy was sleeping. We woke him and his

eyes looked doped, but when I explained to him what I was doing he nodded. "I'm going to show you some mug shots. If you see the man who burned you, nod your head. Okay?"

He nodded groggily. I showed him a random mug shot and his eyelids drooped. The male nurse prodded the victim's foot and he roused, shaking his head at the photo.

The second photo was the same. The third was William Norris. Searcy's eyes opened like saucers when he looked at it. But he didn't nod, and this close to death he was unable to speak.

"Do you recognize this man?" I finally asked, but his eyes just seemed to get wider as if in horror. He finally nodded. "Is this the man who burned you?" I asked as his eyes drooped again, and he nodded. I looked at the nurse with a relieved smile.

****

The next morning, while I was home asleep, a

Zone 5 officer received a call of a burglar inside a labor pool on 3rd Street Downtown. Arriving on call, he met an employee who said he opened up and saw a man on the floor in the lobby. Stepping cautiously inside, the officer saw the sleeping man on the floor and nudged him. When his sleepy face shot up the officer recognized him from my BOLO flyer and grabbed William Norris and handcuffed him.

I was called at home and went immediately to the jail to interview Norris. First I called the Grady Burn unit and was told Searcy was still alive -- but barely.

In the jail I Mirandized Norris. "You want to tell me about it?" I asked.

"You tell *me* about it," Norris said. I could immediately see he'd been through the system enough times that this charge didn't bother him. His dark skin bore the wounds of a hundred street fights. I knew I wouldn't get any cooperation from *him.*

"Slim's still alive," I said, but Norris didn't budge or make a sound. "He ID-ed you as the one who burned him in the van. I also know about the argument you two had over that stolen bike." Norris slowly nodded his head, like it was all coming back to him. "The attendants at the Gulf station also ID-ed you as buying gas there." He was still silently nodding his head. "Norris, I also know you woke Slim up after you threw that gas on him. You stood over him holding those matches." He stopped nodding and began fidgeting, shifting uncomfortably in the hard, jailhouse chair.

"Okay, man," he blurted. "Me an' him been arguin' an' he was drunk an' I told him that when he sobered up tomorrow to be ready because I was gonna kick his ass."

"What about setting him on fire?"

"I ain't got nothing more to say," and the interview had to end there.

****

Searcy died the next day and I upgraded

Norris' charge to murder. His case was bound-over to Fulton County Superior Court.

His lawyer filed a motion to suppress the evidence, which the judge ruled against. The lawyer was a pale, middle-aged man with thick glasses that grotesquely magnified his eyes. He angrily grilled me on the stand as though I were the murderer and his client, by being arrested, was unfairly treated.

When it went to the jury, I spoke to the prosecuting attorney in the corridor. "What's this attorney's problem?"

The muscular, black ADA, wearing a gray suit, rolled his eyes. "He's a white liberal crusader for homeless black males. I heard he left a prestigious law firm to further his crusade. It's like a religious thing for him."

"I wonder why he lacks the same zeal for the black males who are the murder victims."

The jury deliberated for only one hour before declaring Norris guilty of murder. He was sentenced to life.

THE BLEEDING HOUSE.

The entire morning watch Homicide squad, on the night of September 9, 1987, was together in the office eating homemade cake and watermelon, celebrating one of the detective's birthday.

Around 1:30 A.M. the phone rang. Sergeant Jake Turner answered it, and his words immediately made me push my cake aside and listen. "Blood's doing *what?* Coming out of the *walls?"*

An image of Poe's short story *The Cask of Amontillado,* in which the victim is walled up in a wine cellar, came immediately to mind.

"There's no body?" Jake repeated. When he hung up the phone, I asked him what the call was. "An elderly couple called the fire department about blood coming out of the walls of their house. That was a Zone One officer, on the scene. She says there's blood everywhere but no sign of a body."

"How do the old folks explain it?"

"They *can't*," said Jake, furrowing his eyebrows.

Jumping to my feet, I said, "Send *me*, Jake."

****

When I arrived at the two-bedroom house in a quiet black neighborhood in northwest Atlanta, the weather was so clear that I could easily see the full moon.

Inside the tidy home were curious cops and paramedics from the fire department. Sitting calmly in stuffed chairs in their living room were Alma Bailey, a 77-year-old retired school teacher, and her 79-year-old husband Tom.[I've changed these names.]

"See the blood?" Officer Valencia Hudson said, pointing to the carpeted floor.

Hunkering down, I saw what appeared to be a striation of dried, dark red liquid. Being a Homicide detective, I had seen plenty of blood. As far as I could tell, it *was* blood I was looking at.

Following the trail, I walked into a small hall. The living room carpet ended and the blood continued along the wooden floor. In the murky light I saw great splatters and pools that looked like drying blood.

The trail led into a musky-smelling bathroom saturated, floor and walls, with what looked like blood.

I followed the red pools into a back bedroom. If there was no one killed or injured here, this would be the most amazing thing I had ever seen. If it wasn't a hoax, I thought, reminding myself that Halloween was next month. And there *was* a full moon out tonight.

Walking from the bedroom, I stepped into a second bedroom. "I thought the old couple live alone," I said to Officer Hudson, a short, black woman.

"They do," she said, looking quizzical. "They have separate bedrooms."

Trouble at home? I wondered, scribbling notes into a steno pad.

Following the trail, it led through a breakfast room and terminated in the kitchen. At the back door was a concentrated pool and an array of splatters.

Opening the locked back door, switching on the yellowish light outside, I saw more dark spots on the cement porch. This drew me into the yard. Shining my light around, I went to a sawed-off whiskbroom leaning against the wall. Picking it up, I felt that the bristles were wet. Holding it close to my brown eyes, illuminating it close-up with my flashlight, I detected one or two tiny specks of red.

Returning the whiskbroom to its original position, I said to the officer, "Maybe someone squirted the stuff through the floor. Let's see if there's a basement."

Descending a few cement steps cut into the

earth, I found a door with an unlocked padlock. Removing that, we stepped into a dugout basement. Examining the dirt floor, I announced, "Here's more." Next to a television on a stand, there was another pool of blood. "I'm calling ID," I told the officer, unclipping my handie-talkie from my belt.

Later I would learn that an APD radio dispatcher, listening to the unusual radio transmissions from this home, had called a friend who worked for one of the local news stations.

****

Working Homicide, I had discovered a trait among several shooters living in housing projects. They often hide their murder weapon in the washing machine. So, as I was walking back through the Bailey's kitchen, I opened her washer.

Sitting alone inside were two women's bedroom slippers. Carefully lifting them out with my fingers, I could see red splotches across the toes.

****

While awaiting the ID tech, I returned to the living room to interview the elderly couple.

Lowering my skinny frame into one of their stuffed chairs, I pleasantly introduced myself to Alma and Tom. Despite there being a sofa, they both sat apart. Well, I thought, old folks like these would have their favorite chair.

"Could you tell me how this whole thing got started?"

"Well," said Alma, calmly, like she was telling me how she preserves peaches. "I had just taken a bath. And when I was getting out of the tub I noticed what appeared to be blood shooting out of the bathroom floor like a fountain."

"Where were you at that time, sir?"

Mr. Bailey, a twig-thin old man, answered, "I was asleep in my bedroom."

"Mrs. Bailey, can you show me how high it was

shooting up out of the floor?"

Leaning over her armrest, she held her hand about an inch above the carpet. "I thought maybe the blood was coming from him, so I ran to his bedroom. When I ran into the hallway, the blood started shooting up all around me out of the floor."

"How is your eyesight, ma'am?"

"It's fine, and I *know* what I saw."

"Has either of you ever experienced anything like this before?" I asked casually, testing whether they might be senile.

"Definitely not," she said, although I noted no feeling of insult from my subtle questioning of their sanity.

"Are either of you superstitious?"

"No."

"Don't believe in voodoo?"

"No," she repeated, almost as if suffering a fool.

I had seen a lot of blood splatters in my career. There's an entire school of science that has studied the traits of blood as it splatters. With this knowledge, a lot can be determined about the nature of the wound, the height from which it fell, and other marvelous things. From my experience, the blood, if that's what it really was, had not bubbled up like a fountain, as Mrs. Bailey described it. The fluid had been flung on by something -- like a whiskbroom, like the one I had found, its bristles wet from possible cleansing, leaning in the dark back yard.

"You're sure, Mrs. Bailey, that the blood came up from the floor like a fountain?"

"That was exactly what happened."

Listening to this conversation were four befuddled fire department EMTs. To them I asked, "Did any of you guys check the Baileys for wounds?"

"We did," a lieutenant said. "There's not a scratch on either of them. Mr. Bailey told us he's a dialysis patient, so we were especially careful to see if he was hurt and maybe didn't realize it."

Turning back to Mrs. Bailey, I asked, "Has anyone been hurt in this house recently?"

"No."

"Okay, ma'am, what happened after you ran into the hall and the blood shot up from the floor all around you?"

"I went into my husband's room and immediately awoke him and told him to come see what was happening."

"Mr. Bailey, what did you do, sir?"

"I got out of bed and came to see what she was talking about," the frail old man said.

"Did *you* see the fluid shooting from the floor?"

"No, I came out and saw the pools all over the floor."

"So, you yourself *never* saw this fluid doing anything but lying there?" I reiterated, thinking a definite pattern was emerging.

"It was just lying there in pools on the floor."

"How did you react when you saw all this blood all over your house?"

"I immediately called 911. Then the fire department came out."

"So *you* called 911, Mr. Bailey?"

"Right."

"Mrs. Bailey, whose slippers are in the washing machine?"

"Mine."

"I looked at them a few minutes ago and they appear to have blood dribbled on them. Do you know how that might have happened, ma'am?"

"They had been resting on the floor when the blood started gushing and they got splattered."

Might *she* have been wearing these slippers when *she* splattered her own walls with this red fluid? I wondered. Not wanting to sound accusatory, I said, "I also saw a wet mop in the kitchen."

"Yes."

"How did that get wet, Mrs. Bailey?"

"I had left it outside and it got rained on."

"How'd it get back inside the house?"

"I wanted to mop up the floors, but a fireman told me not to disturb anything."

"What did you do after you awoke your

husband?"

"After I checked on him and saw that he was all right, I then thought maybe a pipe had burst, so I went to the basement. I checked there but I couldn't find any broken pipes. When I went out the back door, I noticed the blood all on the kitchen floor."

"Had the house been locked?"

"Yes. No one could have gotten inside, and I know what I saw."

"There's a tissue in the commode in the bathroom, and a tissue in the kitchen garbage can, that both have red liquid on it."

"I'd wiped a small amount of the blood up."

There was a knock on the front door and all the firemen, cops, the Baileys and I looked there.

ID tech Depina, a black female who would later become an investigator for the Medical Examiner's office, had arrived with her camera.

****

During my career as a newspaper reporter, before joining APD, I had chased down numerous stories of haunted houses. Like Nietzsche, I feel it's important "to believe in things, whether we believe in them or not." In other words, wonder adds substance to human life.

This episode, I felt, was a hoax. Who did it, I could not say, though I felt the evidence, and the facts I learned by interviewing the old couple, indicated Mrs. Bailey knew more than what she was telling us.

Depina told me the rumor was spreading among personnel at police headquarters that there was something supernatural going on in this house. In fact, she told me not to leave her alone in the basement, where I directed her to take photos of the "blood" on the floor. "This house gives me the creeps," she admitted as the camera bulb in her hands flashed over the red pool.

"It *sounds* creepy, but I don't feel any `psychic force' here," I said, teasing. "There's no demonic-possession feel at all. Before it's over, I'll have de-mystified this case."

When she was through photographing all the fluid, with closeups to show the splatter patterns, I asked her to take samples of the stuff to send to the state crime lab for analysis.

****

Convinced this house had not been visited by demons, I set about trying to find an earthly explanation. I felt like a wino looking for cans as I searched the Bailey's garbage can on the street. If I found an empty bottle of, say, fake Halloween blood, that might be used to make the perpetrator of this hoax confess.

All I found in the can was garbage.

****

Word about the "bleeding house" was

spreading. Curious Grady EMTs stopped by, parking their ambulance out front with the cop cars and fire department truck.

"I hope you don't mind, Detective," the white EMT with a curly brown goatee apologized, "we just wanted to see what's going on out here."

"What's going on out here," I said, "is that I'm trying to prove this is a hoax. This doesn't even smell like human blood." A Homicide detective notices these aromas.

"What do you think it is?"

"I wish the hell I knew. I'm sending swabs to the crime lab. But they won't have any results for at least a week."

"Well, I can take a sample down to Grady's serology lab. They're not the crime lab, but at least they can confirm it's not real human blood."

"That's a good idea. Let's do it."

Watching as he took a syringe to suck up a specimen from a pool in the bathroom, I noticed the fluid had taken the consistency of the top layer in a can of latex paint. "*Real* blood doesn't congeal like that," I stated triumphantly.

****

"It's real human blood," said Grady lab tech Maria Vint.

I couldn't believe it. After leaving the Bailey house I drove to Grady and walked into the lab on the first floor.

"It's definitely real blood and probably human blood," Vint said. "Your crime lab can do a more detailed analysis."

****

At the Homicide office, I tickled the computer keyboard, trying in vain to find any previous "hoaxes" or false calls at the Bailey house. There were none.

By this time, it was dawn. My shift would end in an hour and I still had not eaten.

Sitting at my desk, before I could bite into a tomato sandwich, the secretary buzzed me. "Cartwright," she said. "A news camera crew is out front. They want to interview you about the bleeding house."

****

The Bleeding House.

That's what the news media dubbed it. It became the lead story on every local news show for days. Every talk radio show had callers voicing their explanations, most of which were supernatural.

So many curious people called Homicide, seeking our official explanation, that an entire phone line blew. My fellow detectives, who had their own heavy caseloads to work, were angry with me for all these calls.

Reporters made the story more bizarre, and I was ordered by Hollywood, my lieutenant, not to speak to the news media about this. *He* would handle the press.

I was hanging up on callers from *Unsolved Mysteries* and other shows. Book proposals were in the mail, all of which I tore up and threw away.

A buddy of mine, who had quit as a Grady EMT to work for big bucks on an ambulance in Saudi Arabia, mailed to me a Saudi newspaper. The Bleeding House was the front page story.

****

The state crime lab confirmed our specimen was human blood, of a type different from either of the Bailey's.

My lieutenant wanted the press frenzy to go away. He turned the investigation over to a day watch detective, who acknowledged to me that he was to "resolve this so-called bleeding house incident."

He, like me, could not find out where the blood came from. He even checked blood banks, but, due to the emerging AIDS epidemic, blood was guarded as tightly as money. None was missing in any blood bank in the city.

The lieutenant told the press that, after a careful investigation, there was no crime his detectives could find. The case was officially closed.

Slowly, the press turned to other topics.

However, almost ten years later, friends still brought up the topic of the Bleeding House.

****

I and Whale still jogged, but seldom together anymore. I started work at midnight when his shift was ending. Sometimes, like this night, we jogged on one of my off-nights.

We were dragging-butt back to our personal cars after a two-mile jog around the reservoir. Whale, a towel draped over his shoulders, said: "Let's do another mile, Cartwheel."

"You're crazy. I'm going to Manuel's."

"Wimp. Manuel's, huh? I thought you've had enough *spirits* lately."

"Do you think the Bleeding House was caused by spirits?" I asked seriously.

"Who knows? Do you?"

"When I was a reporter, in the early days at least, I would've accepted a supernatural premise. But I've grown skeptical. I'm *still* looking for a ghost story I can believe is true."

"We've lost our old-timey faith in God."

I stopped, there in the night beside the whispering lake. Ronnie stopped, also. "What's faith in God got to do with ghosts?"

"It's got to do with ghosts, and UFOs, and even *Star Wars* movies. Don't you see, Cartwheel?"

"No. But I'm sure you'll tell me what you're babbling about."

"Our society's grown cynical. That old time religion doesn't spellbind us anymore. So to take its place, we become fascinated in ghosts and aliens and other supernatural events."

We started walking back to our cars again, silent, in thought.

"You've changed your perspective," Whale finally said. We were almost to our cars. "It's like what I've gone through being a sergeant. I've got to see the administration's views of police work as well as the street cop's. I've got to keep a lot more people happy than when I was just an officer. My perception had to change. It's only when you start to serve that you see the world doesn't revolve around you. You don't understand."

"Like when a cop gets into a shootout? To the administration, they'd rather see him killed -- the insurance will cover that -- than to see him kill a perp and have the perp's family sue the city for big bucks. That what you mean?"

"Something *like* that."

Suddenly a raggedly-dressed black man, his eyes full-moonlike, stumbled toward us from the darkness. Looking at us with his bizarre eyes, he exclaimed: "You got a artificial leg?"

He was obviously a 24, so we walked past him and got into our cars to leave.

****

A few years after the Bleeding House investigation, I read in the obits that Mr. Bailey had died of natural causes. It was surprising he hadn't died that night when his wife stirred him awake, screaming that there was blood shooting from their walls.

KILLER JUDGE.

Briskly walking into court room number two on the second floor of the municipal court building, I expected to see judge Andy Mickle. Instead, I saw Fred Tokars on the bench.

He was listening to a case as I walked up to him. "When did you become a judge?" I whispered. "Aren't you still an ADA?"

Leaning toward me, the skinny man who reminded me of Ichabod Crane, whispered back: "I've been a city judge about two years. I'm usually in traffic court. So, how you doin', big guy?"

"Can't complain. I've got a burglary warrant I need signed," I said, sliding the arrest warrant to him across his lofty desk.

As he read the warrant, the officer testifying before him stood silent.

When Tokars signed the warrant and pushed it back to me, he asked: "Is that okay?"

I figured he was kidding. After all, he had been a trial attorney with the DA's office for years. Now he was a judge. Certainly he knew how to sign a warrant.

But, looking over the warrant, I saw that something was wrong. "You need to sign it at the bottom, and date it here," I whispered, pointing to the correct places on the legal document.

Taking it back, he signed where I indicated, then pushed it back to me. Then I looked into his eyes and saw a disoriented look that alarmed me. "Thanks, Judge," I whispered. "Good luck."

Two days later his wife was murdered by a man who had kidnapped her and the couple's two young sons. She was shotgunned in the head in her vehicle while her kids watched.

Months later, watching the TV as Judge Tokars was entering court in leg-irons and handcuffs, arrested for taking a contract out for his wife's murder, I realized the reason he was so disoriented while signing my warrant. He knew about the pending murder. He was apparently planning it.

SATAN CALLING.

A burglary is akin to rape -- a violation, an intrusion of your personal, private inner sanctum. Your home is where there is peace and security. The burglar brings chaos and sometimes violence. It isn't fair. Crime in your own *home?*

It was around 4:00 P.M., April 6, 1989, when I received a call from a Dekalb County Youth Squad detective. "Have you recently had a bizarre kind of burglary on Lenox Circle in Buckhead?"

"Not that I remember."

"Oh, you'd remember *this* one," he said and I didn't like the ominous tone in his voice. "There should be senseless property destruction and devil - worship graffiti. Maybe something worse."

"Sounds like you have some suspects in mind."

"Escaped mental patients from GMHI [Georgia Mental Health Institution on Briarcliff Road in nearby Dekalb County] . Juveniles. Real sickies. No telling what they may have done."

"Let me check and I'll call you back."

A computer check revealed nothing. I sifted

through the most recent reports that might not yet be on the computer. When that revealed nothing, I called Sgt. Ronnie Shaw in Zone 2.

"I haven't heard any 42 calls today," Whale told me. "Let's go check it out. It's a small street and maybe nobody's home yet."

The sinister way the Dekalb detective described these escapees made me fear what may have happened if someone *was* at home when these particular burglars came calling.

We rode to the neighborhood in Whale's patrol car. Lenox Circle was a small street off Lenox Road in northeast Atlanta. The brick houses, a polite distance from each other, sat in well-tended lots. At this time of the day several home - owners were apparently away at work. We checked the first house for any sign of a break - in, then moved to the next.

I knew that this posh neighborhood was vastly different from the Atlanta Whale knew growing up. Ronnie's mother raised him in a housing project in the shadows of the state capitol building, whose gold dome juts unreachably high into the skies. His mother was a simple country woman transplanted in the big city. She once told her son: "Ain't nobody landed on no *moon!* Moon ain't even *out* tonight!" And she was serious. Ronnie, a child at the time, watched helplessly as a traveling Bible salesman tried to rape his mom. His dad was probably off somewhere chasing some drunken floozie. In this rough life, Ronnie and most of his playmates had one of two fates: becoming cops or being busted by cops. By now, Ronnie had a college education and a wife and daughter in the suburbs. He was also about to be promoted to lieutenant. Things seemed rosy for the ex-high-school football player. He and I were again jogging together at the city reservoir after our shift.

"I think we've found it, Whale."

As we approached the rear of the next house on Lenox Circle, I could plainly see SATAN RULES painted on the rear sliding door.

The plug of chewing tobacco made Ronnie's

jaw appear as if he'd been punched. He spit a streamer into the lawn, then eyed the windows of the brick house for a moment. "Let's find the owners, Cartwheel, and see what we can find inside."

Checking with a neighbor, we were told the owners of the house lived elsewhere while they were renovating this house. "Can you call them?" I asked. "Tell them there's been a break - in, and can they meet us here?"

There was no sign of forced entry and the satanic graffiti was painted from the inside. We didn't know whether any of the burglars were still inside or not, so when the owners arrived, Whale and I, guns drawn, entered the house to search it. The victims waited with the neighbor in case of trouble.

What we found inside was outrageous.

On the rear picture window was painted FUCK YOU!, SATAN RULES, EAT ME, SAVE THE COW, and a crude pentagram.

The entire house was trashed and paint thrown on every wall and floor. More profanity and satanic slogans were within including a huge, encircled pentagram painted on the living room carpet. The words SATAN RULES snaked around it.

In the master bathroom we found a painter's razor and what appeared to be sheared human hair in the sink.

The mattress from a baby crib had been dragged onto the floor and ruined with white paint in the master bedroom.

In the hallway we discovered fresh, naked footprints in the dust. We followed it across the parquet floors to the basement door. Might one or more of the burglars be lurking down there?

With guns drawn, using our flashlights, we descended the stairs cautiously, trying not to foolishly walk into a trap with armed burglars.

But we found no one hiding, only more vandalism. It was safe to let the couple into their house. They moaned with despair when they saw what had been done to their new home. The husband, a senior vice president with the Arthritis

Foundation, wearing a three-piece brown suit, would later estimate the damage was in excess of $16,000.

The wife, in tears, found construction putty and a TV dinner from their fridge had been zapped in the microwave, destroying the oven.

"Who would *do* such a vicious thing?" she exclaimed.

"I think we might have some suspects in mind," I told her. "I'll get back with you when I know more." An ID tech was summoned to take crime scene photos, after which Whale drove me back to my detective car.

Calling the Dekalb County Youth squad detective, I told him, "We found the house, all right. And they did a number on it." I relayed the information to him. "Now tell me what *you* know."

Three juveniles were doing time at GMHI for substance abuse when they escaped from the institute. They were Nicole, 15, Pamela, 16, and Anthony, 15. The detective had captured them in Forest Park and was transporting them back to

GMHI. The juveniles were sitting in the back seat of the unmarked car; he could hear them giggling and talking about breaking into some house on Lenox Circle in Atlanta. He never Mirandized them and did not ask them any questions about the Atlanta burglary.

One of them said Anthony forced the back door open with a screwdriver and Nicole reached in and unlocked the door. Then it was party time. Realizing I had to interview these kids, and knowing what a tricky legal problem juveniles present in Georgia, I called GMHI to make arrangements.

The next afternoon I drove to the huge facility, with its rolling lawn, and met their psychologist, who would sit in on the interviews.

"Have they been told I'm coming?" I asked.

"No," said the doctor.

"Good. I want to interview them separately. If they're in their group it's not likely they'll cooperate with cops."

"I agree."

Working on my degree in psychology at Georgia State University, I was interested to see what made these juvenile delinquents "tick."

Nicole was first. She was led into the psychiatrist's office and introduced to me. Her ravenblack hair looked oily, and her pudgy torso seemed stuffed into her AC/DC HIGHWAY TO HELL☐ tee-shirt. Mirandizing her from memory, I told her I was working the burglary on Lenox Circle. At first the girl denied knowledge, then I pulled the crime scene photos from their manila folder. Hoping she would be proud of her "work," I held up the shot of the graffiti on the back window. "Who did this, Nichole?"

Her face lit up like a child's at Christmas. "Lemme see! Lemme see!"

Looking through the 8 x 10 color glossies, Nichole began giving me a running tour of their senseless rampage. "This is Anthony's hair in the bathroom. Me and Pam painted this. And this." The girls, then, had done most of the painting.

The trio had been walking up the creek that ran

behind the victims' house. Climbing out of the creek, they saw the house looked deserted and decided to break in. "Pam and Anthony did the words and symbols on the sliding glass door," she said proudly. "I believe in the devil. I don't believe in God. I wouldn't be in all this mess at home if there was a god." She taciturnly said she was abused at home, then silence lingered in the air.

Pam was interviewed next. Like Nichole before her, the girl with stringy brown hair and a brown mole on her left cheek denied any knowledge of the burglary until I showed her the pretty pictures. Like Nichole, she was proud of what they had done. They even wanted to know if they could have copies of the crime scene photos.

As she pointed out the graffiti she had painted, she told me, "I didn't mean to hurt anybody. We just wanted to have fun." They are a budding Manson family, I thought. They showed no remorse. It had been fun. "Nichole said we ain't gonna break into it, we're gonna borrow it [the victim's house] . "

Pam said the ice cream in the freezer was "frostbit" and that she ate candy bars they found there, and Anthony "fried the microwave."

When she looked through the stack of photos, she fingered through them again, eyes gleaming as she found special ones. "Nickie is afraid of Jews," she said idly, without explanation, and I realized these type kids probably have little explanations for anything. "When Nickie saw the neighbors next doors were Jews, Nickie ran in fright."

"Why did you do this, Pam?" I asked.

"I just did what everybody else was doing." She told us that the trio had planned to escape from the Dekalb detective as he was driving them back to GMHI. "While he was driving, I was trying to pull my hands out of the handcuffs."

When Anthony was ushered in, the predatory look in his dark eyes was eerie. It was like having a snake stare at me. A chill crawled up my spine as I realized this one could never be reformed. He had already started on a trail of crime and violence. What can be done with a boy like this?

He, too, denied any knowledge of the burglary until I showed him the photos. Like the two girls before him, he became alive, looking at the glossies and bragging about which ones he did.

"Why did you do this, Anthony?" I asked.

"Pam and Nickie had already started, then I just joined in," he answered with no trace of remorse. They had stayed inside the house a few hours, during which time all three of them made long distance phone calls on the victim's phone.

After looking through the photos, Anthony neatly stacked them and placed them on the table.

A month later, as I walked into the crowded waiting room at Fulton County Juvenile Court, a tall woman in overstuffed denim jeans caught my eye. Across the room she smiled and batted her eyes, flirting with me. She had the look of someone with a trailer park as an address.

As I sat there waiting to testify in this hearing, I thought about what one GMHI counselor had said about this trio. They report coming from abusive, unloving homes. "They lack any kind of subtlety," he said. "They just react, they have no self - restraint."

Victims of abuse, terror at home, I was thinking, trying to envision their home environment. These "monsters" are scared, vulnerable kids. When they painted all that Satan graffiti finally *they're* the ones who were doing the scaring, not vice versa. They know adults look at these words and devil symbols and gulp. It gives these kids a sense of power in a life where they have been power*less.*

When I was summoned into the hearing room, I saw Nichole, Pam, and Anthony. I also saw the tall woman who had been flirting with me in the waiting room. She was the mother of one of the defendants. When she realized who I was, as I'm climbing into the witness stand, she blushed and dropped her head.

There were no fathers in attendance at the hearing.

It was then I realized stronger than ever who

was letting down these juvenile "monsters."

ANTICIPATION IS THE HARDEST THING.

Freaknik '95 was only a few days away and the pending confrontation was heavy in the news and on my mind.

It started as some black college students getting together in a local park for spring break. Spike Lee featured it in one of his movies and it suddenly became gigantic, growing each year. Last year it attracted more than 200, 000 kids and paralyzed most of the city. You see, the kids liked to cruise Downtown, but the streets weren't set up for such a street party. Citizens had been complaining and it became a big issue. There were horror stories such as emergency vehicles not being able to get to calls, weddings where groom and bride were trapped and immobile, people's front lawns being used openly by pissing young men, and one vivid incident I recalled where a young woman was having open sex while another guy let her fellate him. This was in the middle of Ponce de Leon Avenue in daylight on the trunk of a car while the crowd cheered them all.

Bill Campbell spent his first Freaknik as mayor out of town, which incensed several locals who became prisoners over the weekend in their own homes. Atlanta was considered a black mecca and its government projected itself as liberal -- but the citizens and local press were howling mad. The mayor had to do something. The festivities before '95 had been wide open -- the outnumbered cops pretty much had to let the kids do whatever they wanted. Now, however, Campbell sent the word out that this year would be different. The kids were welcomed, he said, as long as they did not break the law.

The reaction was revolutionary. Kids in black

berets, wearing FUCK BILL CAMPBELL tee-shirts, made it known they would come to Atlanta with confrontation their agenda. They felt aggrieved that the city would infringe on their "right" to party. The ones I saw interviewed never expressed a concern for the citizens of Atlanta who became victimized by this licentious gridlock.

So we cops were being mobilized, ready to take care of business. For six days our off-time has been canceled. Every cop would report in uniform and work twelve-hour shifts. The state patrol was also mobilized, as were other metro departments. The National Guard was on standby.

I've been in riots before, and it looked like I was about to be in another. We'll be outnumbered a hundred to one.

If I'm injured, who can look after Al, the red-pelted beast I keep in my house? The same dog I depend on to keep out burglars would also keep out any friend or family member who tried to enter to bring him food.

The anticipation of a dangerous detail is often tougher than the actual realization of the event. One is speculation, the other is action. Dread versus physical danger, but at least in the actual event you can act. And that's better.

Fifteen years before, when I worked Zone 2 FIT, a snitch reported two dilaudid dealers we had been investigating had mentioned the next time we raid them they planned to shoot it out.

"Let's hit their place this Saturday," Gene Lassiter, my partner and fellow target, said. "The snitch says they'll have D's in by then." D's were what the addicts called dilaudid, a synthetic type of heroin that was big with redneck dopers.

We had three days to anticipate what sounded like a pending violent confrontation.

My girlfriend tried to cheer me some, even suggesting I make an excuse not to go on the raid.

"I can't run from this thing," I chastised her. "It's my job. It's my responsibility."

When Saturday arrived, Lassiter and Larry

Moore, in plain clothes, rolled by the Downtown apartment building where the dealers operated from. Their mission was just to see how things looked prior to the raid. Things didn't work out that way.

While in the parking lot, the two dealers drove up. They didn't see Larry and Gene who reacted by getting behind them.

"Don't move, Luke," Larry said, jabbing the barrel of his shotgun against the perp's head. That simple, the arrest was made. Guns and D's were confiscated without even a cuss word flying.

Maybe Freaknik '95 will diffuse that easily, I thought, sitting at home, rubbing Al's ears as he slept, his paws twitching as the pooch no doubt dreamed innocently of chasing some cat up a tree.

WOLF SHAMAN.

A black blur leaped from the open door, white fangs turned almost immediately to pink tongue.

Seeing Whale's uniform, the twenty-year-old brunette gasped and exclaimed: "I'm sorry! I didn't know you were the police -- and with the trouble I've been having . . . . Buster! Come here, boy!"

"He's fine," I said, on one knee as I played with her big, black dog.

"I can't believe he's being so friendly. He bit the mailman last week."

"I have an uncanny rapport with dogs. I'm Detective Cartwright. I'm investigating your burglary. Hey, Buster. Hey, buddy."

"You really *do* have a way with dogs."

"See this ring?" Holding out my left hand, the pretty woman eyed my ring depicting a turquoise and silver whirlwind. "It's Cherokee. Some of my ancestors were Cherokee. I figure the reason I have this uncanny way with hounds is because, in a past life, I was an Indian shaman. There was some kind of wolf-shaman thing going on. Dogs descended from wolves, you know."

"Oh, boy," mumbled Whale, and I looked up at his chubby face as he rolled his eyes. "Ma'am, I'm Sergeant Shaw. I'm assigned to the zone out here. I'm assisting Detective Cartwright on your burglary."

Buster and I were still playing. It's true, this canineophile business. I couldn't count how often we've gone out on raids, in housing projects or rough neighborhoods, and a barking dog has charged us. Don't shoot him, I would say, extending my hand. In a minute I've made another friend.

On one raid, I made friends with a mangy mutt, then all her cousins arrived and joined my clan, as well. When I had to leave, they followed me to my cop car and I never saw them again.

"It's nothing cosmic, Cartwheel," Whale declared after we conducted the burglary investigation and were driving off in his patrol car.

"What're you talking about, Ronnie?"

"Your rapport with dogs. It's just because you smell like a dog and look like a dog so they just think you're one of their own."

"Har, har, har," I drolled.

"Did I ever tell you about the time I was a patrolman? The GBI was looking for an escaped convict and me and three other APDers were assisting."

"You've told me this a hundred times."

"Well, I'm gonna tell ya again, so shut up. One of the cops put a dog leash on me and said `Fetch the perp, Whale-boy! Fetch the perp, boy!' The GBI agents were looking at us like we were twenty-fours."

"You *are* a twenty-four."

"And you're a Chihuahua shaman."

"Shaman THIS!"

Police work can be fun working with someone like the Whale. So Fate stepped in, as it seems to do so often with Ronnie Shaw. He was promoted to lieutenant.

We were still huffing three nights a week around the waterworks lake. I'd dropped fifty pounds, due also to a diet heavy on veggies and light on meat. The strain of having worked morning watch for almost two years was also a factor. I had been hidden away in the night like a mole. A lot of my old buddies were shocked to see me with my usually-rumpled clothes flopping over my thin body. Now that I was working evening watch Burglary, some of my old routines returning, so was some of my weight.

"You been sick?" everybody was asking.

"Sick of morning watch. I couldn't sleep. You ever try finding vegetables at four in the morning?"

But Whale, despite jogging three times more than me, could still be called Whale. His face was still cheeky and jovial, contrasting with the sinister look of his grayish crewcut and black SWAT fatigues. When he was promoted to lieutenant, they transferred him from Zone 2.

Soon I was jogging alone. Other cops joined me, but soon grew tired of hoofing it.

So, with all the jogging, why hadn't Whale lost

weight like me?

"Cartwheel, I just discovered a recipe for Swiss steak," he bubbled to me when I ran into him after a barricaded-gunman had been flushed out by Ronnie's squad. "It's so good it'll make you want to slap your mama."

And it returned to me, all the times we'd eaten together on the job: Whale ecstatically digging into a greasy fare of three or four chilli dogs, onion rings, french fries and jumbo milkshake.

Whale was a foodaholic.

WHALE'S SWAN SONG.

On October 9, 1992, SWAT Captain Ronnie "Whale" Shaw took his team out in a helicopter assault exercise.

Flying over the cityscape at night, seeing the

streets delineated by its fluorescent lights, and also the beams of cars, and blue flashes from his brethren on the earth, Ronnie was preparing to repel onto the top of the City Hall East tower.

A sudden wind shear sent his two-hundred-forty-pound body smashing into the roof. A SWAT officer sticking his head out of the hovering helicopter heard what he thought was a gunshot. It was, in fact, Ronnie's knee shattering.

The great irony was that Ronnie didn't have to jump, but figured that, as the CO, he should do what his troops have to do. Come what may.

His injury was massive, but he refused to take a medical pension. He kept telling his doc that he could still handle the job. Raised in that Downtown housing project much of his life, Ronnie always wanted to be an APD cop.

He was reassigned to Zone 1 and suffered through several knee surgeries and therapy. An avid jogger, he could now only walk, and then in great pain. "If some perp started shooting," he told me, "I couldn't even duck for cover under a table."

Ronnie's doctor, no doubt impressed by his determination, let him stay on the job. But the knee wouldn't get better and it was apparent he would have to get it replaced. Whale still wanted to remain a cop, but acknowledged his injury made him physically unfit. He would have been satisfied with a permanent office assignment. But it was not to be, and in '94 Whale, who had been with me on so many of my investigations, was pensioned with a medical.

He'll never forget being on his back on top of that tall building, looking up into the blackness of space, seeing the moon like a giant eye looking down at him.

THE STOLEN RENOIRS.

My theory of how this almost - million - dollar art theft was an insurance rip-off made sense. At the time.

The Zone 2 officer radioed that he needed me at a townhouse on Peachtree Road in Buckhead to investigate an extensive burglary of an oil painting collection. There I met Dolores Sutton [I'm not using her true name], a middle-aged widow who had brown hair clipped close to her skull. She told me she had been out of town two days. Returning home on March 23, 1994, around 6:40 P.M., she found a dozen oil paintings stolen from her walls. Many of the frames were antiques, and two Renoirs made the total loss $800, 000.

"Do you have an alarm system?" I asked, hearing what sounded like Vivaldi playing in the next room.

"I do."

"Did it go off?"

"No."

"Let's take a look at the control box." I followed her to the basement / garage and to a closet where the unit was hidden. The wires had been cut and pulled out.

"The alarm has a thirty - second delay after any door other than to this closet is opened," the victim explained. "If the code isn't entered, the alarm will go off in thirty seconds."

That meant the burglar was familiar with the alarm system in her three - storied townhouse.

"And there's no sign of forced entry," said the uniform officer.

"Who, besides you, has a key, Ms. Sutton?"

"My maid and a friend. I trust them both."

"I'm going to look at your front door," I said.

"Don't let my cats out," she said and something struck me as odd here. Using my flashlight, I scrutinized the front lock for any sign of tampering. None. I also checked the garage door to the basement where the victim parked her Mercedes. No sign of tampering there or along her windows.

Reentering the townhouse, I examined the paintings lining the walls, and gaps where the stolen ones had been. One of her cats rubbed my ankle.

As I checked the front door to see if it had a

spring that would automatically close the door behind a fleeing burglar, I sensed Ms. Sutton thought I was not buying her story. My experiment proved the door would have remained open if it had been left that way. The cats would have escaped. In my notes later that night I would write: "One of my theories: `nice' burglars stole 12 big framed pictures, but never left the door open so v's [victim] cats could escape." TV's Lt. Columbo would have been proud of me for discerning this!

"As soon as you supply me the complete list of the stolen paintings, I'll send a flash bulletin to all metro police agencies," I told her before leaving.

At the Burglary office, I left a message with the victim's alarm company that I needed to speak with the owner. As a precaution, I ran the victim's name through our computers to see if she had a criminal record. She didn't.

When she alerted her insurance company about the burglary, they immediately assigned an investigator. He was retired from APD and we knew each other. With Ms. Sutton's approval he ran a financial check on her. If she were in debt that might suggest a motive for an insurance rip - off. When the investigator called me with the results of that check, the theory of a fraud flew out the window like a bird. "She's quite wealthy," he told me. "She owns a thriving business and her husband left her a hefty trust fund. Besides, in talking with Ms. Sutton, she treats her paintings almost like her children."

She got the list to me quickly and I distributed them via teletypes to all metro police departments. I also contacted the local FBI who alerted their agencies in other large cities. The agent was aware of international fences of stolen paintings currently under investigation, and agents in charge of those investigations would be notified.

And still no response from the owner of Ms. Sutton's alarm company. That made me suspect them. The insurance investigator had a similar theory: In his interviewing Ms. Sutton, he discovered she had a third Renoir, and it had not been stolen.

He and I grew interested when we learned the third Renoir had been moved just prior to the burglary. It had been replaced with a lesser - known painter's work and *that* work had been stolen. Might it be that the alarm installer had made a list while there of where all the most valuable paintings hung and given the list to a burglar? Might that explain why the third Renoir was not taken?

Then the investigation took a remarkably ironic turn. Ms. Sutton phoned me with information from her art broker, Ms. Stabler. Ms. Stabler had received a call from one of her other customers, Mr. Hall, about someone approaching him about buying two Renoirs. I immediately phoned Hall.

"I received a call," he told me, "from a young man who said `You might not remember me, but my name's Tom Tarpley and I used to be employed by ---- Alarm company. I installed the alarms in your home four years ago. While I was there, I noticed you had several nice paintings. I just inherited two Renoirs and I'd like to sell them for cash.' I told the man I'd check with my art broker, and I took his name and number. Ms. Stabler tells me she thinks they're stolen."

We traced the telephone number to an address on Creatwood Circle in Smyrna, a town north of Atlanta. It was not listed to a Tarpley. I ran Tarpley's name through our computers but couldn't find a criminal history. I did find he had a driver's license and the twenty - six - year - old suspect listed his address as Creatwood Circle.

Calling Mr. Hall, I asked if he would arrange a meeting with Tarpley. He phoned the number and Tarpley answered on the first ring. A stakeout of the meeting location was put together, with cops posing as construction workers. We waited and waited but no one showed.

By this time my boss, Lt. Overstreet, who would be murdered in only a few months, had gotten interested in the case. TV's Lt. Columbo investigates murders and supposedly is a lieutenant because he's such a good detective. That's not how it goes in a real police department. The rank of lieutenant is an administrative position, not an investigatory one. Lt. Overstreet, none-the-less, took an active role in this investigation. He covered the day watch and I took over from four to midnight. But we were both in on the stakeout, which was finally called off when Tarpley failed to show.

Mr. Hall, a tall, fiftyish man in a Brooks Brothers suit, kept calling the Tarpley number but was getting the answering machine. Finally, later that evening, Tarpley answered and Mr. Hall wanted to know why he hadn't shown up, that he was a business man and he had wasted an entire afternoon.

"I got confused about the directions," Tarpley said vaguely.

"I'm still interested in the Renoirs."

"Well, I found out they're fakes."

"How?"

"I took them by Sothesby's."

"You went to *New York?*"

"No. They have people all over the world."
Tarpley didn't want to talk to Hall any more and hung up.

This put us in a dilemma. Was Tarpley faking us? At hearing that we weren't going to be able to lure Tarpley into our jurisdiction with the paintings, Lt. Overstreet suggested we get a search warrant for his home in Smyrna.

"But if we do that, and he's got the paintings stashed somewhere else," I said, "he'll know we're onto him and we may *never* get the paintings back. We don't have even a shred of evidence against him yet."

So we decided we'd quietly work on Tarpley for a few more days. If that didn't succeed, we'd go ahead with the search warrant.

I contacted the FBI and arranged for their surveillance crew to watch Tarpley's house. They had helicopters and planes and all sorts of play toys APD lacked. Our Intelligence squad started the paperwork needed to get a wiretap put on Tarpley's phone.

We feared if we made a wrong move that alerted the suspect to us, he could destroy the paintings before we had a case on him. Lt. Overstreet, his muscular build not disguised beneath his gray suit, went to visit one of Tarpley's neighbors at her work place the morning after the stakeout. He identified himself, telling her we were looking for stolen paintings. She immediately looked nervous and asked if he had pictures of these paintings.

Overstreet drew the Polaroids from his jacket pocket. When she saw them, she looked horrified. "Tom's been storing these paintings in my basement," she exclaimed. "I had no idea they were stolen." She was so upset that she gave Overstreet a key and told him it was her house key, and for him to please go there and get those paintings out of her garage. However, she gave him the wrong key. He couldn't open her front door and Tarpley's condo was attached to hers, and Overstreet stood just ten feet from Tarpley's front door.

Using his police handie-talkie as he hid behind the house, Overstreet had the APD dispatcher call the neighbor and explain that she'd given out the wrong key. Luckily, she had a key hidden outside and Overstreet was soon inside her home. Yet when he opened the garage door, the paintings were gone.

"What are you doing here?" a voice behind him challenged. Turning, Overstreet was face to face with the suspect, Tom Tarpley. His short black hair looked uncombed, like he'd been napping. *This,* thought Overstreet, is the mastermind that pulled off one of the most expensive residential burglaries in the city? The blond lieutenant, towering over the finicky-looking suspect, felt like he could have huffed and puffed and put the little guy in the wind.

"I want those paintings back," Overstreet growled, jutting his gold badge in Tarpley's face. "We have evidence linking you to them. Give them back now and we won't put you in jail."

"*What* paintings?" Overstreet glared at Tarpley. Trembling slightly, Tarpley muttered, "You promise you won't lock me up?"

"I'm not in the habit of lying, Tarpley."

The skinny suspect took the lieutenant to his bedroom, and there were all twelve of the stolen paintings. With a sense of triumph, Overstreet radioed to the office: "Call Cartwright at home and have him meet me up here ASAP."

When I arrived an hour later, Tarpley was locked in the back of a Smyrna police car. I Mirandized him and he told me his story. Or, rather, parts of his story. My investigation would fill in the blanks that would implicate Tarpley in this and other high - value burglaries.

Tarpley was an independent alarm - installer and paper - hanger. He had hung the wall paper in Ms. Sutton's townhouse. While doing so he became upset with her when she made him redo a room. It was then he plotted his revenge for this slight. While alone in the townhouse, Tarpley went to the garage and unscrewed the remote - controlled garage door - opener. There he noted the dip switches before screwing it back together. Later buying the same brand garage door - opener, the wily thief set its code for the dip switches in the victim's system. This was how he gained entry while Ms. Sutton was out of town. And this was also why there were no signs of forced entry and why her cats had not escaped through an open door during the burglary. He simply loaded his booty into a vehicle parked inside the closed garage.

Also while alone in the victim's home, hanging the wall paper, he studied her burglar alarm. Using his knowledge of alarms, he knew he would have thirty seconds to enter the garage, go into the closet and cut and pull the appropriate wires. Then he could remove the paintings at a leisurely pace and he would have his sick sense of revenge fulfilled. Besides, he'd own some nice art.

"Why didn't you show up at the meeting with Mr. Hall?" I asked.

"When I drove to the address, I saw a Mercedes that looked like the one Ms. Sutton drives.

I thought she was on to me." But that Mercedes belonged to the art broker.

"Have you done any other burglaries, Tom?" I asked.

"No," he said. Within two days I would prove this a lie.

We removed the paintings from the condo where Tarpley was staying with a male friend.

As promised, we gave Tarpley a copy of charges for the oil painting burglary. We transported the paintings to police headquarters where then - Chief Eldrin Bell was so elated at the happy ending of this unusual burglary that he held a press conference. One of his last before retiring from APD.

When Tarpley arrived at municipal court for his preliminary hearing, I arrested him for a second burglary. This time, despite having no prior criminal history, he was held in city jail with no bond.

While investigating the Sutton burglary, I came across a burglary at an antique store on North Highland Avenue NE. This had not originally been assigned to me, but the owners suspected Tarpley although there was no evidence. However, it fit what I then knew was his MO. He had been employed here, but was fired and swore he'd get "revenge." So very similar to his experience in working for Ms. Sutton.

There were no signs of forced entry into the warmly - lit antique store, a large shop overflowing with blue crystals, chiming clocks, cloth dolls, and stone figurines. I assumed that, while employed, Tarpley made a copy of the key. Stolen were several fine antique items. Having seen Tarpley's possessions, I realized he liked the finer things. He also liked stealing them. The stolen items were things he had expressed a liking for while employed there. Hidden keys had been removed to get into locked displays. Keys that Tarpley knew the location to. But I needed proof.

A lady who'd seen our press conference called me at Burglary. "Tom's an acquaintance," she said. "He knows I collect nudes, and he sold me an art deco lamp made from a nude figure. Could he have stolen that, too?"

Meeting her at her office, she showed me a pewter lamp. "Is it stolen, too, you think?"

Pulling a Polaroid photo from my antique store file, I showed it to her. There was no doubt. Now I had my physical evidence in the second burglary and I wasted no time in securing an arrest warrant for Tarpley.

The store co-owner was the ex of my first APD partner. Despite *that* unfortunate revelation, she was delighted to see her lamp returned.

"What's its value?" I asked.

"She's an import from England, one of a kind in the States. It's worth $800."

"Tarpley sold it for $200. Told her he found it in a flea market."

"*Right,*" she laughed, running her palm along its smooth contours.

Another worried friend of Tarpley's called me next. He said Tarpley had phoned from jail and asked if a detective had contacted him.

"I told him no, and he told me to get rid of that stuff he'd given me. If this is stolen, Detective, I don't want anything to do with it." I went to his apartment in nearby Gwinett county and discovered the bulk of the $18,000 worth of property stolen from the antique store. Now I had two solid burglary cases against Tarpley. But was there even more he had done?

Going through other Buckhead burglaries, looking for Tarpley's unique MO, I soon charged him with a residential burglary from prestigious Peachtree - Dunwoody Road. He was hired to install a man's alarm and had gotten angry with him. More Tarpley revenge.

My witnesses and victims were afraid of Tarpley, despite his being a small, effeminate person. They spoke of him like he was a ghost, able to float through walls, defeat any alarm system. At the prelim, the victims and witnesses asked the judge to order the TV cameras there not to reveal their faces.

He was bound over for trial in Fulton County Superior Court and kept under no bond. The Assistant DA assigned the case agreed that Tarpley was a risk, and in August 1994, Tarpley copped a plea to these burglaries. He was given a sentence of ten years in prison, where he'll have to do without the finer things he had enjoyed for such a brief time.

OLYMPIC BOMBING.

When the bomb went off at the 1996 Olympic Summer Games in downtown Atlanta, I was underneath it.

All off-days had been suspended for us to secure the Olympics in our town. We worked 12 hour shifts and I was assigned to a unit securing the dignitaries' entrance to the Omni, where the volley ball games were held. My unit worked with a military unit that was mostly responsible for checking every incoming vehicle for bombs. I preferred being outside where there would be more action. I only entered the Omni to watch the Brazillian female team play; they had high-cut tight shorts that were ... inspiring.

Part of the Omni was under a viaduct; this was where I was when our radios erupted excitedly with voices alerting us a bomb just exploded on the viaduct above my head. Realizing re-enforcements were needed, I ran to my sarge and volunteered to take half our unit topside while the other half remained on post. For all I knew, we were under attack by terrorists.

On street level, we ran for the location of the explosion. All of the civilians were running away. The crime scene was pandemonium and we began moving the crowd so ambulances could transport all the wounded. A woman I ordered to move out of the street looked down her nose at me and declared: "You can't tell me what to do!"

"Get out of the street so the ambulances can get the wounded to the hospital, or I'm putting you under arrest!" She looked like I'd slapped her, but she moved out of the way of the emergency vehicles.

As law enforcement brought order to this chaos, I realized there were no terrorists to fight. A pipe bomb had been left in a backpack and had exploded, killing two people and wounding more than 100.

Being a detective, I knew precious evidence from the bomb had been trampled on, so when I spotted screws, nails, and wadding, I straddled it to preserve it for subsequent analysis.

A man near me shouted: "All non-federal personnel are ordered to immediately leave this crime scene!"

I called back to him: "I'm preserving evidence!"

"Exit this crime scene!" he snapped to me. "WE'LL find all the evidence!"

The feds were taking jurisdiction of the crime scene, so I reluctantly returned underground, my adrenaline still pumping.

GIT-TAR MAN.

"Hold onto your hat, Cartwright, but I think our git-tar man might be about to surface again." I immediately recognized the voice over the phone as Detective Rick Mavity of the Nashville, Tennessee Metro Police Department. This burglary of vintage Gibson Les Paul electric guitars was one I thought I'd never solve. Then came the break in the case.

"How do you know it's the same guy?" I asked while untangling the phone cord.

"He contacted Hill again. By phone. Told Hill he had twenty git-tars for sale and would he be interested."

"I'm not aware of any burglary in Atlanta of so many guitars," I said. "Do you have any in Nashville?"

"No. But he stole 'em *some*where."

Hanging up the phone, I watched the cord coil back together like a caduceus.

So far this crime stretched 239 miles from Atlanta to Nashville. The phantom burglar had used different names: "Bob," "Daniel Johnson," then "Bob Irwin."

Running the names through every computer application at my disposal, I still did not have the burglar identified.

This multi-state investigation began on June 11, when a neighbor of Joshua Stanford's called APD to report an audible burglar alarm.

A lone female officer arrived on the call. The alarm was still ringing and she could see a small dog running around inside the middle-class home. A raised window bore pry marks.

When the victim arrived, he examined his house. "Oh, God, they've stolen my guitars!" Valued at $5,500 a piece was a 1992 Gibson replica of a 1959 model, and a reissue of a 1959 model.

"This seems like the burglar knew what he was after," I said to the victim. "Do you suspect anybody?"

"None of my friends would have done this," he said. Then an idea struck him. "I advertised in the paper to sell these guitars. One person showed up."

"Did he tell you his name?"

"He did. What did he say? Oh yeah. He said his name was Bob."

"No last name?"

"Just Bob."

"Can you describe him?"

"He was a white guy around thirty. He really knew his guitars."

"Did this Bob say anything about where he lived?"

"No. In retrospect I think he was being pretty secretive."

"Did he come to your house in a car?"

"Yep."

"Did you get a tag number?"

"To be honest, Detective, I didn't really pay that much attention."

"So, how did your meeting with `Bob' end?"

"He declined to buy my guitars. Said I was asking too much."

"And you say no one else responded to your ad?"

"No one."

All I had was a first name and a MO of a burglar who answered ads for expensive vintage guitars, then came back and stole them.

Stanford visited every music store in metro Atlanta. He left a copy of the serial numbers, which I also entered onto the FBI's NCIC computer network.

A few days later, Stanford phoned me at Burglary. "Some guy called a vintage guitar shop up in Smyrna. Luckily, I'd already talked to this store so the owner asked for a description, including the serial numbers."

"You don't think a question like that might scare the burglar?"

"Serial numbers authenticate a guitar as vintage."

"Okay."

The caller identified himself as Daniel. Contacting a Smyrna detective, we planned a trap for `Daniel.' But he didn't cooperate by falling for it.

Stanford phoned me two weeks later. The Gibsons had surfaced in a Nashville guitar store.

"How did *you* find that out?" I asked my victim.

"I already gave that store the serial numbers."

That struck me as curious. Why would my victim in Atlanta call a guitar store all the way up in Nashville?

Phoning Nashville PD, I was lucky enough to reach Detective Mavity. I explained to him about the stolen guitars, then expressed my suspicions.

"You don't know much about vintage git-tars, do you?"

Surprised, I admitted my ignorance as I again tried to unbraid my phone cord.

"Gibsons are manufactured here in Nashville.

It's only logical a vintage pair like this would end up here."

"You see a lot of these kinds of thefts?"

"Yep. And I also am a Gibson owner. You ever hear the song `Nashville Cats'?"

"Sure."

"The music scene's big in Nashville. We got a lot of musicians here trying to get their big break. When they're down on their luck, a lot of 'em have to sell their instruments."

Mysteriously, my phone cord remained uncoiled. That afforded me extra space to hover over my desk as I pieced together my notes.

Within an hour Mavity called back. "I've confiscated those Gibsons. An' man are they beauts."

"Do we know who sold them to the store?"

"Yep. A guy named Archie Hill."

Scribbling his name into my notes, I said: "So Archie Hill's my suspect."

"Nope," said Mavity. "I've already talked to Hill. He bought 'em from another guy."

"Did Hill get a name?"

"Guy left Hill a receipt, handwritten, signed `Bob Irwin.'"

The description of `Bob Irwin' fit the description of `Bob' who had answered my victim's newspaper ad prior to the burglary.

"How did `Irwin' get in contact with Hill?" I asked.

"Hill has an ad in a local paper saying he buys vintage git-tars. This Irwin guy called and arranged a meeting at one of our malls."

"That's his pattern," I said. "Responding to newspaper ads about vintage guitars."

"This Irwin guy," continued Mavity, speaking as though he knew the name was an alias, "brought the git-tars to the mall. They haggled, like this Irwin guy knew what he was talking about, then sold them for $3,250. Hill thought he was getting a real good deal. Now he wants to know how he can get his money back."

"We've got to catch the bastard first. I'll run

this name through our computers, but I'm sure he doesn't exist."

My laborious computer search was in vain, but by now I was beginning to feel the excitement of the chase. We were getting so close . . .

Then the burglar made his fatal move. He called Hill again, wanting to sell him twenty more guitars.

Mavity was as excited as I was when he called me with this. "Do you think Hill will cooperate in setting this guy up?" I asked.

"Hell yeah! He realizes it's the only way he'll get his money back."

Then began the waiting game for our illusive prey.

Mavity phoned a few days later. "This Irwin guy called Hill. Asked him to call him back in half an hour at 432-3171. Can you trace down that number?"

"I'll get right on it. Call me back when you hear from Hill."

The number was traced back to a pay phone

on the first floor of trendy Cumberland Mall in nearby Cobb County. Contacting mall security, I asked that they do surveillance of this phone and I gave them `Bob Irwin's' description.

Nothing.

Much later that night Mavity called. "Hill called the number but nobody ever answered."

Had our phantom perp spotted the surveillance at the mall and ditched his plans?

Two days later, Mavity phoned again. "He just called Hill. Gave him a different number -- 955-9838."

"Why is he playing all these cat-and-mouse games? You don't think Hill's pulling our chain, do you?"

"Hell no. Hill's nervous, but he wants his money back."

The second number was traced to a pay phone booth at a Dunkin Donuts. Calling a buddy, a Cobb County detective, the unknown geography was explained to me. "That doughnut shop is next to

Cumberland Mall," he said. "And not far from the guitar shop your `Daniel' called on the phone."

We were getting closer to the burglar.

On July 26, Mavity called. "The Irwin guy just called Hill. Wants the deal to go down tonight at a mall in Nashville. I'll be there watching."

I could only sit at my desk in Atlanta while the sting went down -- or didn't go down -- in Nashville. Someone other than me was taking care of business.

Part of my job as a newspaper reporter had been drawing cartoons. Now, as a cop, most of my case notes and file folders were festooned with cartoon doodlings. This particular folder more so than usual.

When Mavity phoned, I could hear the triumph in his voice. "Your perp's <u>real</u> name is Robert Daniel Dubose, DOB one-fifteen-fifty-nine."

"You snatched his ass?" I exclaimed.

"He's in the Nashville jail. Had sixteen more vintage guitars with him."

"His name -- Robert is Bob, the name he used

with my victim, and Daniel is the name he used at the Smyrna guitar store."

"Yep."

"Did he make a statement, Mavity?"

"Not at first. But he finally admitted, after I told him what you and I *know,* that he answered the newspaper ad in Atlanta and had gone to Stanford's house. Of course, he denies stealing them, but I can put him in possession of them up here."

"It's convoluted, but it's a good burglary charge. You might get a free trip to Atlanta for his trial."

"No, thanks. I don't like visiting Atlanta. Nashville's all right enough for me."

Awaiting Dubose's extradition, I began tracking down the sixteen guitars the burglar had with him when arrested by Mavity.

Cobb County had just such a burglary. Calling the detective in charge, I asked: "Did your victim advertise his guitars in the paper?"

"He sure did. But how did *you* know?"

SPAM, SPAM, SPAM!

I was hungry working an extra job in uniform, watching the dawn sun reveal downtown Atlanta around me.

I could not sit or leave my post, so I watched a Spam truck set up near me. Soon the smell of Spam cooking began to tease me. I kept telling myself Spam is junk, probably not even edible. I watched as tourists went to the truck and ate samples.

When I was finally able to take a break, I went to the truck and happily sampled fried Spam, with melted cheese, with fried onion, on a muffin with mayo. Best food I've ever gorged on!

WHAT☐S SO FUNNY?

The Audi ran the red light. I hit my brakes to keep from crashing into the bastard. He just looked at me and laughed as he sped on. It seemed like he was just another Atlanta AOW, Asshole On Wheels.

"It's times like this," I said to Sam Coleman, a fellow Burglary detective, that I wish we were in a patrol car. I'd pull him over and give him a ticket. We were just returning from doing a search warrant.

"It's a sign of the times," Sam, who was nearing retirement age, replied.

"Well, I'm going to run his tag," I declared, falling in behind the speeding Audi.

"I'll do that. You drive." Sam reminded me of Bill Cosby, often wearing sweaters and sniffing due to a sinus condition.

The Audi zipped in front of a red car, cutting it off without signaling as Sam radioed in the tag number.

"It's a symptom of a bigger malaise," I groused.

"Yep," agreed Sam, whose perspective on life often mimicked a preacher's. "Jaywalkers and people like him have no respect for others."

"They're just self-centered assholes. Look at him. He just cut off *another* driver. Looks like he's laughing about it."

"He *is* laughing."

"Fifty-one-thirty-six," the dispatcher transmitted. "That tag's a Code 19."

"Start a Zone car, Radio. We're southbound on Peachtree Street approaching 3rd."

I stayed up with the stolen Audi until I saw blue lights in my rearview mirror. "Radio, advise the Zone cars the Code 19 is the silver Audi directly in front of my unmarked blue Taurus."

Two patrol cars pounced on the car like predators. When the Audi stopped, we all stopped and leapt to the street, our 9mms trained on the perp.

"Put your hands up!" I yelled at the driver, a young black male. He quickly complied and I yanked open his door and pulled him out.

Once we cuffed the perp, I told him: "It's pretty damn stupid to drive like a maniac in a stolen car."

"He doesn't care," said Sam.

"You a bunch uh chumps," taunted the teenager with all the gold teeth. "Yeah. I stole the motherfuckin' car. I just got outta the joint." He shrugged. "In five month I be back out again."

"It's brothers like you that are dragging society down," Sam told him. That made the kid laugh louder.

The perp was still laughing at us as the paddy wagon drove off with him.

"I'll be glad when I retire, buddy," Sam said as he climbed back into the Taurus. "After twenty-nine years on this job, I deserve to retire and spend time with my daughter and my young wife." Sam slammed the door.

THE ATTORNEY WHO RECOGNIZED A

NAME.

The testimony I gave in a burglary case in municipal court was short and sweet:

"Your honor, on July twenty-second, the home of Tony and Ann Shelton was burglarized and jewelry belonging to Mrs. Shelton was stolen. Those items were a sapphire ring, a diamond ring, and the Shelton's wedding ring which bore the inscription `To my beloved Ann on our wedding day, April 12, 1978 -- Tony.'

"On the same day as the burglary, the defendant pawned those stolen items. The stolen jewelry has been recovered and Mrs. Shelton positively identified them. I hold here the pawn ticket where the defendant pawned the stolen items, putting him in recent possession of the burglarized items. The fingerprint on the pawn ticket has been analyzed by the Atlanta Police Department ID section and I hold here a report from ID stating the fingerprint on the pawn ticket belongs to the defendant."

This was a probable cause hearing and the judge bound the case over to superior court for trial.

In the hallway the defense attorney called out to me.

"I didn't realize until I heard your testimony," he said, "but I know the victims. They're friends of me and my wife. We had dinner with them last weekend! Please don't tell my wife I was this guy's attorney!"

TALE FROM THE CRYPT.

"Why'd they classify breaking into a grave a *burglary?*"

Hearing Hamp Ingram, the race-car-driving

detective, ask that, I looked up from my desk. "What are you talking about, Hamp?"

The short, stocky detective held a report in his hand. He was distributing the last batch of Burglary reports for the night. "This report says someone broke into a mausoleum and stole five skulls. Here. It's assigned to you."

Reading the brief narrative, it appeared a locksmith, Robert Exum, had been hired by a woman in Tennessee to make keys for the family mausoleum. When he arrived at the church cemetery that day in February, he made a startling discovery: "He noticed that someone had broken into the mausoleum and broken into three infant caskets and two adult caskets. There was still remains left and scattered about the mausoleum. I notified Sgt. King of the incident," the report concluded, "it appeared that several skulls had been stolen."

"Why is that classified a burglary?" Hamp repeated.

"The perp entered a structure and committed a

theft. Skulls," I said. "That would make it a burglary, even though I've never worked one like this."

"Sounds like your bleeding house case," he jibed.

"Who would steal skulls?"

"Maybe grave robbers."

"Grave robbers would try to steal valuables, like rings."

"Maybe Satan worshipers."

"This is going to be interesting," I said, looking at my wrist watch. It was almost midnight and the end of my shift. My regular off-days started tomorrow so I couldn't start the investigation for two days. "Damn," I muttered.

"At least you'll have something interesting to talk about at Manuel's tonight."

Hamp was right. At the tavern that night, I announced, "I was just assigned a case where someone broke into a mausoleum and stole five skulls. Three babies' and two adults'."

Whether talking to fellow off-duty cops or

civilian friends, these Manuelites glowed with morbid curiosity.

"Any messages painted on the walls?" a friend asked.

"I don't know."

"Any ransom demands?" a detective asked.

"I don't know."

"Any suspects?" a sergeant asked.

"I don't know."

"You wanna buy a round for your buddies, Cartwright?" the bartender joked.

"Yeah, right."

When I returned to Manuel's Saturday night, the story had circulated. Waiters, waitresses, fellow Manuelites, and the parking lot security guard approached, all asking: "Anything new on the skull case?"

"I don't know. I don't go back to work until tomorrow and the suspense is killing me. I love these bizarre cases."

"This might be better than your bleeding house

case."

"It has potential," I admitted.

Mike Malloy, a radio talk-show host with wild gray hair and black-rim glasses, sat at the bar and fired up a cigarette. "I heard about the skull burglary, Steve. Can I mention it on my show?"

Thinking about it, I said: "That might be a way to generate tips."

"So it's all right?"

"It might also attract nuts who have no knowledge of the crime."

"So what do you say?"

"Can you just make a brief announcement?"

"Sure."

"I'll listen to your show and see what kind of response it gets."

Driving to headquarters Sunday afternoon, I was anticipating getting some answers.

First I contacted the woman in Tennessee. She wasn't much help. "I don't know of any local relatives," she said over the phone. "I know I had a grandfather buried in there, but he was moved to another grave years ago. I'm not really sure who is still in the mausoleum."

"So the bodies are pretty old?"

"Probably over a hundred years."

I called Exum, the locksmith who had discovered the crime. "Are you sure it's not some attack by animals?"

"Couldn't be that. It looks like they may have laid one of the adult skeletons on the floor and snapped off the skull."

"Why do you think that?"

"There's pieces of bone, like the vertebra, on the floor."

"Did anybody clean it up?"

"I left it just the way I found it. In case you needed to search it for clues."

"Good. That's just what I need to do. Can you meet me at the graveyard and let me into the mausoleum?"

"Now? It's Sunday afternoon."

"I want to get to it right away. This is a pretty dastardly crime."

"Okay. I'll meet you. It'll take me forty-five minutes to drive into town."

I requested an ID tech meet me. I radioed Sergeant Bob Adams, a uniform patrol supervisor in Zone 2, and asked him to meet me at the Sardis cemetery. Adams worked with me on several burglaries in his zone, and I knew this would interest him. Since Whale was gone, I'd been collaborating with Adams.

Arriving at the church cemetery in the heart of Buckhead, Atlanta's most opulent community, I recognized the place. The rear of the cemetery was a popular spot for midnight rendezvous for lovers who had just met at any of the several trendy bars on nearby Roswell Road. The back lane was also used by teenagers drinking beer or smoking reefer in the dark.

Tracie Kelly, the comely black ID tech, met me at the mausoleum around five P.M. It was sunny and unusually warm for late February. Waiting for the locksmith, Tracie and I walked the grounds looking in vain for clues. The red brick structure looked more than a hundred years old. Its roof consisted of slate blocks turned black by the weather. The building stood only a few yards from the cars passing on Powers Ferry Road.

A man walking his dog through the church ground eyed us curiously. "Maybe that's our perp," I whispered to Tracie.

"That man?"

"No. His dog."

She grinned.

A patrol car pulled up. "I heard you call Sergeant Adams," he said as he approached. "I was wondering what a Burglary detective was doing in a cemetery."

Other zone officers, just as curious, joined us. The sight of patrol cars in the cemetery attracted the stares of passing motorists. A neighbor strolled up, asking, "Is anything wrong?"

"I'm investigating a break-in of the mausoleum. Have you seen anything suspicious out here lately?"

"You know this is a hot place for parkers."

"Yeah. Is there anybody in the neighborhood -- like a teenage boy -- who might be strange enough to break into a mausoleum?"

"Not that I'm aware of. This place has been broken into before."

"Yeah?"

"About five years ago, I think."

"I didn't know that. Do you know if anything was stolen?"

"I don't know."

When Sergeant Adams arrived, there were three patrol cars for gawkers to wonder about. One of them called from their cellular phone to tip off a TV news crew. *Something* was going on at the Sardis church cemetery.

When Exum arrived, it was finally time to enter the ancient mausoleum.

****

The door was black metal, sealed with heavy chain and padlock. Baring entrance to the door was a swinging portcullis. One of its vertical bars was slightly bent at the top.

Opening the lock, pulling off the intertwined chain, Exum pushed open the door. It only opened a few inches until something inside the mausoleum stopped it.

"Let me go in first," I said.

The darkness inside the crypt was interrupted only by the hole in the roof the burglar(s) had used for entry. It was covered by a twisted piece of aluminum.

My eyes at last accustomed to the creepy darkness, I saw what was blocking the door. It was a coffin lid lying in the middle of the room, upside down. Atop it was a plastic Kroger bag containing something big.

Three walls contained shelves made of pipes.

There were two tiers. To my right, a coffin sat on the concrete floor. It looked ancient and had a glass faceplate that had been shattered. Above it was a second adult coffin whose glass plate also was shattered.

Stepping over the coffin lid on the floor, I saw three wooden baby coffins in the top left corner. Jagged pieces of wood jutted from the top where they had been pried, but I could not see the top.

As Exum had described, what might be pieces of vertebrae rested on the bottom coffin, and on the dirt floor.

Tracie entered and took photos before I disturbed anything in my examination.

Sergeant Adams, short and thin, unlike Whale, his predecessor, asked: "Did you see this crow bar?"

"The one in the corner? Yeah," I said. "We've got pictures of it."

"This Kroger sack doesn't look like it came from the eighteen-hundreds," Sergeant Adams quipped blackly. "I wonder what's in it."

"I'll open it once I'm through examining these coffins," I said.

Peering into the shattered glass of the coffin on the ground, I saw a chaos of bones and wooden debris. "That looks like the ribs," Adams said, looking over my shoulder as I shined my flashlight into the violated coffin. "But no skull. I don't see a skull."

"Neither do I."

Shining my light into the adult coffin on the first tier, I saw its inhabitant was less disturbed. "Tracie. Try and get a picture of this skeleton. I can see an old dress and a spinal column sticking out of its collar, and a round indentation in what's left of the pillow. But no skull. There's no doubt. It's been stolen."

"What sick mind would do a thing like this?" Adams muttered, darting his light around the dark crypt.

"With this angle," Tracie said, examining the coffin, "to get a picture inside, I'll have to stick the camera inside with my hands. I won't be able to see to focus."

She estimated the focus, then stuck the 35mm. through the tight space. The flash was like a quick, blue lightning bolt.

"I'm going to climb up these racks and look into the baby coffins," I said, and hefted myself carefully up, lest the ancient ironworks break and tumble the three pathetic coffins down on our heads. It was like climbing monkey bars in a playground. "Okay. I can see the top of all three coffins. There's a wooden coffin that's been broken, but inside is a metal coffin and they're all intact. So they *didn't* steal the baby skulls."

The crime scene investigation was complete except for one last thing. "Tracie, could you get some plastic gloves from the ID van? I'm going to see what's wrapped inside this Kroger bag."

Donning gloves, I carried the bag outside, back into the sweet light of day. A small crowd had gathered, mingling with the curious zone cops. Placing the bag on the ground outside the crypt, the locksmith's wife said to their two children: "See, kids? It's just like on TV."

Cautiously peering into the Kroger bag, I saw it contained a second plastic bag. Removing this, I noted it was a plastic Eckerd pharmacy bag. Inside that was another plastic Kroger bag. Inside that was a large, zip-lock freezer bag folded once. When I unfolded it, one of the locksmith's kids gasped.

"Better get a picture of this, Tracie." The bag contained one long human bone, like an arm, and two smaller bones like vertebrae.

****

"I wonder if the sick bastards dropped that bag?" wondered Sergeant Adams.

"Or if they left it where they did for a reason," I said.

After we left, the local TV news crew, tipped off by a caller, arrived. Not seeing any cops, they left, thinking the tip had come in from some prankster.

****

The hot topic on Mike Malloy's radio show Monday was over federal spending. He didn't get a chance to bring up the vault story.

A few nights later I saw Mike at Manuel's. "Did you catch the show yesterday?"

"I missed that one, Mike."

"Well, I brought up the topic but no one called."

"Oh, well."

****

A detective called me, said he had heard about the bizarre theft. There had recently been some church vandalism in nearby Cobb County where Satanic symbols had been painted on the church walls. "Do you think your case might be related?"

"I don't think so," I admitted. "There were no

signs painted, no black candles left burning. I'm wondering if this could be a college prank or just the work of some sick kid doing it for his own pleasure. Vandals are usually saying `Look at me!' This seems more private."

"Satan worshipers usually steal finger bones," a Homicide lieutenant told me. "I don't think real Satan worshipers use skulls."

"That's odd. Fingers instead of other bones. I wonder why."

He shrugged.

"Maybe the skulls were stolen by a bowling league," I quipped darkly. "You know, bowling balls?"

****

There was no end to speculation. On my next off-day I read where a horror convention was being held at the Sheraton Colony Square Hotel in Midtown. Phoning my office, I spoke to Detective Tony Volkadav, who resembled Clark "Superman"

Kent. "Clark," I asked, "will you buzz by that convention and see if any sick puppy there has any real live human skull?"

"That's stretching it a bit, don't you think?"

"Stretching's all I've got right now."

Alice Cooper, the '70ies shock-rock star, was supposed to appear at the convention. He had to cancel, but sent this message to the thousand fans of the 1995 World Horror Convention: "I slipped and fell into an open grave and was accidentally buried alive last night."

The dapper detective looked out of place among the black-clad, pasty-skinned conventioneers. Several of them sported vampire fangs; others, heads shorn in Mohawk hairdos, were wearing tee shirts emblazoned with lithographs of famous American serial killers.

But he found no one with any purloined skulls.

****

No suspect has ever been unearthed in this bizarre case. (Sorry about the pun. I can't help myself!)

Joking, I asked several fellow detectives to join me inside the cold mausoleum on a stakeout. "Just think," I said. "We're hiding inside when they come back. Once they're inside, I jump out and GRAB 'EM! They'll think their victims are getting revenge. It'll give 'em a heart attack!"

SPACE MAN!

The stench of APD's old HQ building, where the detectives were on the 3rd floor, was worse than a leaky gas mask. By contrast, the men's room in the basement -- that required a key to enter -- seemed almost as lush as the Fox Theatre's restrooms.

A Burglary detective, Charlie Horton, was working late. Charlie was a big brown bear, the friendliest guy I've ever met. He fought in Vietnam as a Marine, and went about doing good deeds; he once told me: "I try to live my life, Steve, as if I'm sending building material to heaven for the construction of my eternal mansion." It was around 1 AM and he thought he was the only living person in the old building as he tucked an AJC under his arm and took the rattling elevator to the basement. When he rounded a corner, he ran into a man in a space suit. But he was not NASA. He was HAZ MAT.

"We're cleaning asbestos out of these walls," the worker told the detective. The City had them doing this without fanfare in the wee hours of the night. All hush-hush.

VISITOR.

Looking into the eyes in the photo, I wondered if murder victims somehow *know* someone is about to snuff out their life.

The photo of our lieutenant was in a folded *Atlanta Journal* I'd uncovered while cleaning out my cluttered desk.

Only a few months ago they had fished the Burglary squad CO out of a South Carolina lake, nude and shot fourteen times with his own 9mm. They arrested his wife. Apparently she didn't take it too well when he told her he wanted a divorce.

Could I see an uneasiness in his eyes? No, I decided. Lieutenant Doug Overstreet was thirty-six in the photo, his blond hair clipped short and neat beneath his blue cap and gold badge. We had received a commendation letter for solving the Renoir burglary. Now Doug was dead.

He had everything to look forward to.

Intelligent, smart with computers, possessing a knack for planning huge events, he was on the 1996 Olympic Planning Committee. Doug had been APD's youngest lieutenant. Rumor was he might soon have been our youngest Deputy Chief.

With his love for this job, might his ghost, among others, haunt this old building? On one wall of the squad room hung a photo of a detective, Bob Tillman, who always had a joke. He was accidentally shot to death by his brother on a fishing trip in the Gulf of Mexico. It's always impressed me that as Bob lie paralyzed and dying, he told his brother he forgave him. His spirit might also want to linger in headquarters.

I was about to be a ghost here. The chief had just transferred four Burglary detectives to other squads. After eight years in this squad room, the CID major told me he wanted me investigating crimes in the city's forty-two housing projects.

Four of us were cleaning out our desks and stacking case folders into cardboard boxes. My new office would be in the Housing and Urban Development building in Midtown. I couldn't help opening files and reminiscing.

"Cartwright."

Hearing the secretary call my name jolted me from my reverie.

"You have a visitor up front," the big black woman said.

Walking out of the Burglary office, down the concrete corridor past the empty lieutenant's office, past the open door leading to CID's deputy chief, it startled me to see Whale waiting for me in the lobby where the elevators were.

"Ronnie," I said, you don't have to wait out here like a visitor -- "

"Yeah, I do, Cartwheel," he said, wearing jeans and a gray sweatshirt. Unlike other retired cops, the forty-three-year-old still kept his hair short and his face clean-shaven. "I don't even think about this place anymore."

"Bull."

"I hear they're moving most of the squads to City Hall East."

"Movers have already started. This place'll be empty in a few months."

He looked at a passing detective without recognizing her. "I was just down here signing some more endless pension forms. I heard about the new transfers."

"Nothing stays the same for long on this job. You know that."

"I haven't been gone but eighteen months, and I swear, I don't hardly recognize *any* of the cops anymore."

I opened my mouth, then closed it and avoided his eyes.

"I guess ya'll'll be celebrating the moves tonight at Manuel's."

"Yeah."

Turning toward the two elevators, he mumbled, "Maybe I'll stop by. All I got now is free time, anyway."

"Do that, Ronnie."

Before he could punch the button with his pudgy finger, one of the empty elevator doors whisked open and I smiled. "Thanks, Uncle Charlie," I said.

Whale cut his eyes my way. "You trying to get a psych-pension, Cartwheel? Talking to empty elevators?"

"I've told you about my Uncle Charlie. He worked in this building in the early-sixties before he retired. Sometimes I think I can feel his presence here. And -- like now -- an empty elevator often opens up for me -- like he's sending it to me."

Stepping inside, Whale looked at me in mock-apprehension until the doors slapped shut between us.

****

Our waitress looked sexy in her tight jeans and brown tee-shirt. The sway of her small but high breasts caught my attention. She wasn't wearing a bra. I noticed all the guys at our table at Manuel's were subtly watching her every move, also.

"I'm in love," a Robbery detective exclaimed. "Why don't I just cut to the chase and write her an alimony check *now?*"

Stuart, a British bobby who was here temporarily on a cultural exchange, clunking his empty beer mug onto the table at Manuel's under the Zone 7 sign, said: "I'm thinking about becoming a U.S. Citizen and putting in to be a copper."

"Why?" I asked, although I could have been asking the same about myself.

Stuart didn't answer. Instead he watched Ronnie Shaw hobble back to the table from the restroom. The Whale's rebuilt knee, smashed in his helicopter leap, obviously troubled him. "Your mate there, Whale you call him, he was forced to retire because of his injury, but he still meets with you all here at the tavern."

"Hardly ever," I answered, pouring another

draft into Stuart's glass.

As Whale lowered his bulk into the chair across the table, Stuart asked him: "Do you miss the job?"

"Sure I do," he said, running his beefy hand through his short, prematurely gray hair. "But I know I can't cut being on the street anymore. With my knee, I couldn't run, couldn't even duck under the table if a perp started shooting." Did Whale seem blue? We used to jog together. Despite his burly size, Ronnie liked to jog two or even five miles a day. Now he sits in front of the tube like a househusband. He and his thirteen-year-old daughter haunt flea markets together, and watch goofy horror films at the last drive-in theater in Atlanta. He who only recently repelled from SWAT helicopters and sleuthed around with me. Now, sitting around our table at Manuel's, Whale was as much a visitor as was Stuart. "I miss the guys. Now I sit around the house and watch bad horror movies. Maybe I can use all this downtime to edit Cartwheel's book."

"Right," I said, then laughed. "The only thing

you read, Ronnie, is the instructions on a box of frozen pizza."

"What'd you say the title of your trash book is? *Diarrhea in Blue?*"

"Still the same wit as always!"

****

Cops from patrol, CID, SWAT, and other assignments, kept arriving around the party table. "Who put that bumper sticker on the wall?" asked a Mounted sarge, pointing to a "YOU BOOK EM, WE COOK EM -- Jackson, Ga." sign on the wall.

"A guard works Jackson comes in here, I said. Pretty funny."

The state prison in Jackson was home of Ole Sparky, the big chair that sparks and crackles.

"Whale!" I called. "Have another beer! I'm gonna put you in my book!"

"I couldn't *fit* into a book," said Ronnie, eyeing the treasures in the menu.

"Whale's a cannibal's wet-dream," I teased, as

his eyes narrowed in silent pain. "Har, har, har."

"Har, har, har, yourself, Cartwheel. Put me in one of your moronic books and I'll sue you."

"Sue *this!*"

Whale's grin turned into a grimace as another painful tic stuck him like a pin.

****

We watched Ronnie hobble back to the table from the restroom. The Whale's rebuilt knee obviously troubled him.The cute waitress slapped down three pitchers of beer as more off-duty cops came in, boisterously calling to their comrades.

"You really think the ghost of your great-uncle haunts the headquarters building?" Whale asked after sipping his beer.

"Well, a few months ago I was in ID. I happened to look down and saw an ancient fingerprint card. Looking at it, I saw it was from 1939. It listed my uncle as the arresting officer."

"What the hell was *that* doing lying around?"

"I asked all the techs how it got there. Nobody knew. I mean, a card that old would have to be in the archive."

"Maybe in the year 2020 *your* ghost and your uncle's will be at police headquarters, mysteriously opening the elevator doors for the next generation of Cartwright cops. Doo-doo, doo-doo, doo-doo, doo-doo."

Next to us, a table of two couples cut nervous glances our way. No doubt they heard our loud stories and realized we were off-duty cops. They looked at us like we were aliens. In a sense, we are, I realized, seeking a stray napkin to jot more notes for the book.

We're different from you, I scribbled, causing the flimsy paper to rip. *I'm driving in to work when rush hour traffic is going in the opposite direction. When you're sleeping, we're patrolling beneath the street lights, chasing perps through dark alleys. While you're flipping burgers on the grill on the fourth of*

July, we're loading bodies into the hearse. Doing good detective work. I thought back, almost two decades to when I first heard the East Point detective use that expression.

Whale stopped my writing by punching me playfully in the shoulder. "I've got another story for you, Cartwheel! I want you to put it in your book."

"Okay, Whale Boy," I jibed back. "But it'll have to be in the next one. One *you'll* read. A comic book!"

"Har, har, har," Whale drolled, subconsciously massaging his artificial knee. "Har, har."

"You wish you could come back?" a voice asked.

"No, I don't."

I knew he was lying, but didn't press it. Maybe later, I decided, again hoisting my beer mug to my mouth. "*What?*" I asked, noticing his quizzical look at my blue tee-shirt.

"`May the force be with you'? In your case, Cartwheel, it should be `May the *farce* be with you.'"

Whale popped a french fry into his mouth, proud of his witticism.

I liked that tee-shirt. I'd chosen it because the phrase from the movie *Star Wars* conjured up the idea of mystical energy *and* the police force.

Once a cop's retired, no longer kicking in doors and chasing bad guys, The Force is gone from him. A cosmic link. You have your memories, but, listening to the loud laughter around our table, I realized a certain energy abandons your body when you pull that badge pin for the last time.

The realization unsettled me, especially so close to Ronnie. I felt like blurting out to my comrades: "Even if I won a million dollars in the lottery, I'd still stay a cop!"

May The Force Be With You. Like some mystical energy, like the stuff of real ghosts, and like it was leaping and arcing in this room tonight.

I looked at Ronnie, realizing that when *I* retired, that force would leap from my body and surge on through younger men and women. While I languished in an old folks home, my memories fading, that force would go on forever, strong and vital, leaping and arcing, leaping and arcing, and leaving me far behind, an ash growing small and cold. A lonely ghost, not even a faint blue light. Maybe I'll haunt APD headquarters like my Uncle Charlie did.

EPILOGUE.

I took an early retirement so I could concentrate on my writing. I was in APD Reserve for years.

I continued the fight of good versus evil by volunteering for dog Rescue. That, as they say, is another story.

My books are available at Amazon.com. Put this link in to your browser: http://amzn.to/2ia1DMT .

A Christmas For Healing.   I was put on Earth to write this story. This is its fourth printing.

Emmett Nagel is a cop wounded in the line of duty. His smashed body has turned his soul dark and cold. Buoyed by his loving wife, Emmett is about to learn that you can't help yourself without first trying to help others.

Rescue Dog Rescue Me 2   Dog is God spelled backward.

Steve Cartwright, a retired cop and former newspaper writer, turned his love for dogs into his passion for dog Rescue. Helping those saved from death row was good for this long-time Rescuer's soul.

Also meet Dog Therapist Barry, so attuned to dogs' Wolf Nature he seemed like a shaman mystic.

Kenna, a saver of abused dogs, often saw them touched by such blessings they could only be bestowed by God.

They work with dogs who need help: Callie started out a trouble-maker but became a brave service dog for a wounded Marine.

Ava snapped at certain people, but time – and love – turned her into a sweet companion.

Jack -- what, or who, made this black lab so terrified? Could Jack be saved? And dozens of other Rescue dogs and their tragic, sweet stories that every dog-lover will thrill to. 168 photos.

Rescue Dog Rescue Me   A veteran dog Rescuer shows you how his way of helping homeless dogs has evolved after he let his first Rescue out of the cage and they, almost all, jumped into his lap. And he learned more: Shelter Syndrome. Lap Therapy. Foster Fail. Volunteers help dogs by loving them, playing with them. The Rescuer is often the first to ever give love to these abused dogs.158 photos.

I Dream Of Oddkins   A new book of surreal cartoons. In it a familiar-looking psychology guy explains about how the Id is like a dark basement in our subconscious. In that basement, things called Oddkins hide, casting our dreams & nightmares on a spinning wheel of magick.

Dark Tales From Gents' Pens (Annie Acorn's Dark Tales Book 1)

Where can you find all the suspense, thrills, blood, and gore that reflect the dark underbelly of our world? Where do murder and voodoo curses stand alongside innocents and little children? Where do the kinder, gentler things disappear? Within the tightly crafted stories gathered for your enjoyment by Annie Acorn into Dark Tales From Gents' Pens!

With their skillfully woven tales, the founding members of From Gents' Pens, a cooperative of award-winning contemporary male writers, have forged a unique collection of stories that are sure to please those who enjoy a tingle running up and down their spines, as they face the monsters who no longer linger beneath their beds.

Contains:

The Halloween Clock by Annie Acorn

The Petrified Girl by Steve Cartwright

The Challenge of the Killer by Steve Cartwright

The Embalmer's Apprentice by Steve Cartwright

The Reincarnation of Lou Gehrig by Joe Eliseon

The Horses of Paiute Canyon by D. A. Grady

The Two Hundred by K. Edwin Fritz

Shelter by William D. Prystauk

Ms. Grant by William D. Prystauk

The Dead and the Dying by Ron Shaw

Made in the USA
Columbia, SC
19 April 2021